Pottery

Tony Birks

A complete guide to techniques for the beginner

...books · A & C Black · London

By the same author:
Art of the Modern Potter
The Potter's Companion
Basic Pottery
Building the New Universities
Meyer's Ornament (ed)
Hans Coper
Lucie Rie

© Tony Birks 1979, 1988

First published 1979 by Pan Books Ltd
This revised edition published by
Alphabooks Ltd, Sherborne, Dorset
A subsidiary of
A & C Black (Publishers) Ltd
35 Bedford Row, London WC1

ISBN 0 7136 3021 3

British Library Cataloguing in Publication Data

Birks, Tony, *1937–*
    Pottery: a complete guide.—2nd ed.
    1. Pottery. Marking – Manuals
    I. Title
    738.1

    ISBN 0-7136-3021-3

The tuba players on page 1 are by Christine Poole

Printed by
BAS Printers Limited, Over Wallop, Hampshire

Contents

Introduction

1
The spectrum of pottery

In the unlikely event of the world's peoples having to start again from scratch, the potter would be at quite an advantage. On a clean-slate Earth, he would not have to look far for his raw materials. His skills do not need a complex technological backup; his product would be at once useful and quite soon a kind of balm. Like the fisherman or the good cook, the modern potter readily takes advantage of the latest offering from modern science, but with a strong sense of improvisation he can come to a *modus vivendi* with his basic materials if all else fails.

Clay is an extraordinarily versatile material, with a capacity to be shaped when it is soft and plastic, and to keep its shape when it is dry. Unlike, say, polythene or rubber, it does not melt or burn when heated up, but instead becomes permanent and stable. Most ceramic, from porcelain to brick, is fairly easily broken – but it is almost impossible to get rid of the pieces.

The heating up or firing of the clay causes irreversible changes in the material and so, for 7,000 years or so, potters have been feeding clay to the fire and producing a mass of expendable

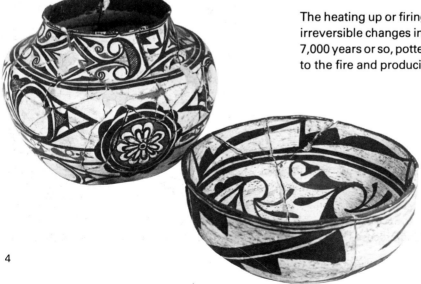

Pueblo Indian pots, made by hand with painted decoration c. 1900

waste and some of the greatest masterpieces of creative art. The modern potter or pottery student can find a comfortable and appropriate niche somewhere in this wide spectrum, and according to his taste and temperament gain increasing satisfaction with experience. Luckily, it is not necessary to start young, as with the playing of the violin, and even more happily, potters do not get feebler as they get older. Pity the poor skier who has to be on the slopes almost before he can walk and is finished by the time he is thirty. Most potters agree that their work gets better with years of experience.

There is a mass of information available to the pottery learner. More books seem to be written each year on the craft of pottery than any other popular theme. The reason why *this* book is being written and is being structured in its particular way is that attitudes to pottery have changed enormously in the last few years, and it seems well worth trying to give an outline of the whole range of techniques available and to encourage potters both experienced and novice to experiment with unusual methods. The experimenter will quickly discover, however, the truth of the adage that there is nothing new under the sun. In methods of manipulating and decorating clay, both for functional and decorative pottery, he will find that other potters, particularly in the Orient, have trodden the same paths – but it does not matter. The process of understanding the capabilities of clay is an infinite one. The basic material is timeless, yet ever new.

Many people come to pottery with set ideas about their aims, some with the very reverse. Most will find, after a short acquaintance with clay in the hand, or a visit or two to a museum of ceramics, that the possibilities are greater than they ever dreamed. The danger facing a new student is that of mixing metaphors; of confusing asymmetry with crudeness on the one hand, or excusing inept clumsiness on the grounds of freedom of expression on the other. Too readily and too often inappropriate techniques are tried for functional pots, or stiff and automatic skills become applied to what should be an organic making process.

Not an ancient symbol, but a modern hand-made ceramic by Ian Godfrey

5

Above: thrown shapes by Hans Coper

Below: giant storage jars in Portugal

wheelmade bowls to representational sculpture and wall mosaics which are intended to delight the eye and senses. There is plenty of promiscuity across the frontier, but some techniques are more appropriate to the first category and some to the other. This book is primarily about techniques, and so in the first section about functional pottery, wheel techniques and casting will be described. In the second, other mechanical techniques and hand-making processes will be found.

It is misleading to separate decoration into its own, third section, since decoration belongs integrally to the pot, whatever its function or technique, and indeed in many instances the technique *is* the decoration. Nevertheless, decoration and glazing can be assessed and described in abstract terms and independently, and the book ends with an oblique approach to this aspect of ceramics.

Sometimes an inspired pot which defies definition will make nonsense of a demarcation between functional and creative ware, but if lines have to be drawn to aid the student, then this is where we shall draw it. On one side will be the pottery which can sensibly be used in the house for containing everything from peanuts or wine to chickens in the oven. On the other side will be the ceramic shapes, from simple

The several experts who have contributed to the book, describing their own skills, sometimes contradict one another, which only goes to prove that there is not, in pottery, one true inviolable way of doing things. There may seem to be further contradictions in Section One and Two and the reasons for this should be obvious – each is aiming at a different result.

2 A new look at clay

Clay is bought in bags, inconveniently heavy for the average person to lift. It is either powdered, like flour or cement, or ready mixed with water to a plastic state and wrapped in polythene so that it stays that way. Prolific potters grumpily object to 'paying for water' and will mix the powder as a baker will mix dough in a large machine, like a giant, slow-motion Kenwood, according to their day-to-day requirements. More modest users stick to the plastic variety and try to remember to seal up the bag so that it does not dry into an uncharitable stone. Powdered clay is, of course, simply this hard block ground up again, for the particles that make it up are very fine molecules of alumina and silica. By adding water to these particles the material becomes plastic, i.e. capable of being moulded into shape and of retaining its shape. With the addition of more and more water this vital plasticity, one of the key properties of clay, breaks down again and the material turns into 'slurry' and finally into 'slip', a thin creamy liquid which one sees flowing in the clay streams from clay mines in such places as Cornwall. The potter can use clay in all of these stages. He can carve into the solid block or create casts or paintings with the slip. Mostly, however, he is making use of the plasticity of the clay when it is malleable but not sticky. Press your thumb into a piece of plastic clay. If it readily takes the impression but does not 'pluck' at your thumb when you take it away, it is probably usable by the potter. If you look carefully at the thumb-print in the clay you will see that it is as precise as a police record-card – which gives a clue to another important property of clay. It is capable of taking and retaining an impression. Thus house bricks show their maker's names, or the delicate patterns of leaves can be recorded permanently; just like plaster of Paris, clay puts you into the reproduction business.

The basic clay molecule is made of alumina and silica, and the clay molecule is lamellar or plate-like. It is far too small to be seen without a microscope, but clay particles take up the plate-like characters themselves, and slide over one another like a pile of magazines. Lubricate a clay hill with rainwater, and it will soon slide downwards under gravity. The more the lubrication, the greater the slide. Centrifugal force, on the wheel, is a force extremely like gravity, and the slipping of the clay particles helps to explain why a pot can be widened on the wheel without cracking up.

A new look at clay

The Raw Material

There are, of course, clays and clays, and this book is not the place for a treatise. They are all naturally occurring, but most of those prepared for the potter are blended, like sherry, to give certain characteristics and to ensure uniformity. Clays can be fine or coarse, but these terms have different meanings to the industrial chemist and the studio potter. The potter is interested in plasticity (i.e. throwability), refractoriness (i.e. fire-hardiness), shrinkage, colour and texture. All these features are inter-related, and clay suppliers adjust the character of their clays by varying the constituents.

Silica and alumina are the main ingredients, roughly in the proportions 2:1. Other elements such as iron, titanium, calcium and potassium may account for only 5 per cent. By mixing natural clays from various sources, different degrees of plasticity are achieved, and very plastic clays have high shrinkage since they contain more water in their structure. The so-called impurities which clays gather when carried by rivers, etc. are very important to their colour. Most clays contain some iron, which makes the orange colour of bricks and plant-pots, and further elements can be added (see Chapter 16), although this reduces the refractoriness of the clay and often makes it unsuitable for high-temperature ware. Additions of sand or 'grog' (ground-down pot) may improve the texture or 'tooth' and will reduce shrinkage, but will also reduce plasticity. You cannot have it all ways and there is no clay which is 'the best'. Once you have got used to one, stick to it. I recommend a plastic white stoneware clay, which can be adapted according to your needs by various additions. If you are buying your own, get it from one of the major suppliers listed on page 133, or direct from Moira Clays Ltd, Burton-on-Trent, Staffordshire. Moira clay has the advantage of making an excellent casting slip (see Chapter 6).

If you have clay in your garden, or a clay-pit nearby, by all means try digging some and testing it for shrinkage, colour, plasticity, etc. Even if it is dark blue in colour it will almost

By adding grog to fine clay, its texture becomes coarse and gritty.

certainly fire red, because of the iron in it, and you will be very lucky if it is clean and plastic enough to throw with. Only put small pieces like dominoes in the kiln for test firing, as garden clays easily blow apart, and if they do, large fragments can damage other pots in the kiln.

If you make use of several prepared body clays, try to keep them separate in the workshop. Do not make the mistake of thinking that by mixing them together in a common wastebin, you will be able to reconstitute a miraculous and personal clay which has the best qualities of each. What in fact will happen is that the carefully constituted bodies prepared to have special characteristics will lose these, and extraneous ingredients, such as metal oxides, drops of glaze and fragments of plaster or sponge may have fallen in, and you may end up with a clay which bloats or explodes. Worst of all, you will never be able to repeat the clay if it does happen to be good, for whatever mixture you have made is unlikely to be the same as the next one which appears in your wastebin.

Clay loses size as it dries, and again when it is fired in the kiln. Total loss will be between 10 and 15 per cent according to the clay, and this makes an enormous difference. It is difficult for the studio potter to make precise calculations, but remember that a jar capable of holding one litre of water when freshly thrown might, after firing to stoneware temperatures, hold only 600cc, which is not much more than a pint. This is one of the reasons why pots which look enormous after the effort of making them often seem so small and insignificant when the firing is finished and the potter has come down to earth. The higher the temperature of the firing the greater the shrinkage, and the pot becomes correspondingly heavier for its size as it gets denser. It is customary to call low-fired pottery earthenware, or software, and high-fired pottery stoneware. Everything depends on temperature. Clay becomes pottery – that is to say, it is chemically changed so that it no longer breaks down in water – when it has been heated over 600°C. It begins to be useful as pottery, though not very strong, from about 800°C. Pottery described as earthenware is usually

The cracks which appear when clay is dried by the sun indicate shrinkage.

The first stage in preparing clay for use by the potter is to slice up the lump and bang the pieces hard together.

fired between 1000° and 1100°C, and stoneware between 1200° and 1300°C, when the clay itself becomes impervious and rock-like.

It is economical of energy to fire pottery at lower temperatures, but the special qualities given to pots by intense fire encourage most studio potters to make stoneware, although many clays will not reach this temperature without distorting or blistering. In later chapters the beginner will be directed to the kind of ceramics which best suits the technique he is learning.

Preparing the clay

Preparatory to potting is the hard slog of preparing the clay to make it smooth in texture and workable. It involves the slicing up and kneading of a lump of plastic clay as illustrated

By pressing down with the heel of both hands on a lump of clay and raising the far edge of the lump with your fingertips, you can create a rhythm which will circulate the clay and improve its consistency. It is important to knead the clay with a smooth rhythm or it will stick to the bench.

Below: use a wire or nylon thread to cut through the kneaded clay in several places. By this means you can check for irregularities within the lump, as shown on the next page.

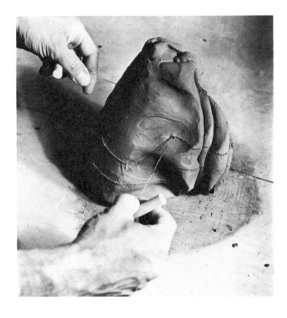

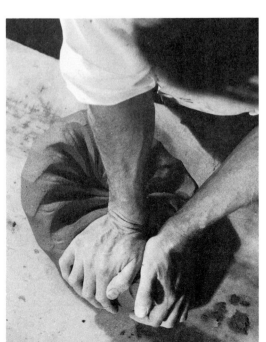

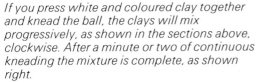

If you press white and coloured clay together and knead the ball, the clays will mix progressively, as shown in the sections above, clockwise. After a minute or two of continuous kneading the mixture is complete, as shown right.

in the accompanying photographs. It is boring, hard work and is made worse if the clay is not in good condition in the first place. If you were to rest your head on your elbow and your elbow on a ball of clay, the clay should be deeply indented by the weight, but not so tacky as to stick to your elbow and come up with your arm. This round-about procedure is not recommended as a regular practice – you will soon learn how soft or hard clay should be in order to be worked on the wheel, or into coils or slabs.

If it is too soft, spreading it on an absorbent plaster-of-Paris surface or a piece of dry, unsealed wood, will help. If it is too hard and leathery, water will soften it up quite quickly if poured into holes prodded into the lump with a hardy finger.

Polythene bags are a great improvement on damp rags for keeping the clay in good condition for weeks and weeks when it has been prepared. Thin polythene is best, and it is important to make sure that the prepared pieces of clay are wrapped tightly and thoroughly. If the polythene is snagged or torn the clay will become slowly but surely dry behind your back.

Balls of clay ready for use

3 Technique on the wheel

The most immediate magic in ceramics is undoubtedly when pots appear in seconds from lumps of clay on the wheel, though the regular thrower is so used to it that magic might seem an inappropriate word. For him it is second nature.

The circular motion of the wheel is used to make objects which are symmetrical. The plasticity of the clay allows the shape to be drawn up. It stretches and, like a rubber band, in doing so becomes thinner. Thus a small spherical lump the size of your fist can become a sturdy half-pint tankard or, in skilled hands, a delicate bowl 20cm across. The most important thing for a beginner to recognise is the inevitability of failure. The woodworker on a lathe can expect some sort of result from his first effort. Not so the pottery beginner. The pots he makes on the wheel will tear and sag and crumple whilst he is learning the characteristics of clay and the limits of its endurance. It is sensible, therefore, to have a good deal of clay ready prepared before going on to the wheel, separated into balls which will each fit easily into your cupped hands. The size of the optimum ball of clay will vary according to the size of your hands. Normally it will be somewhat larger than a tennis ball. Press the ball down on to the centre of the wheel head, making sure that this is dry and that the clay is not sticky. Although you need a bowl of water nearby for lubrication, it is important that you do not wet either your hands or the clay until the latter is firmly stuck on to the wheel head. If you are using an electric wheel, there will be a control operated by your foot or knee, which acts both as clutch and accelerator. So-called kick-wheels (powered not by electricity but by the foot) will have a pedal or treadle linked to the spindle of the wheel head and a heavy flywheel to keep up momentum. Potters' wheels do not go round very fast – one revolution per second in pottery is putting quite a strain on the clay, and is quite fast enough to execute the necessary shaping. The speed of the wheel is relatively fast when you are beginning a pot and should become progressively slower as the pot nears completion. Most of the throwing is done with an electric wheel on half-speed or less.

Students tend to learn quicker on electric wheels as there is less to think about and less body shake. Using a kick-wheel may be as difficult for the beginner as positioning a record player pick-up whilst pedalling a bicycle. Nevertheless a good kick-wheel is preferable to an electric powered wheel with worn bearings. An old wheel which rumbles and rattles and shakes – so that you can move the wheel head from side to side when the power is off – will make learning hard. If there is any choice at all the beginner should use the wheel which runs smoothly.

Most wheel heads have a series of concentric circles engraved on the steel or wood, which helps in the positioning of the clay centrally on the stationary wheel head. The next few stages are the same for every wheelmade pot, but before starting up the potter should have the basic tools within reach. These are a bowl of water, which should be cold or tepid, not hot, a sponge no bigger than a medium-sized potato, a cutting wire like those used for cutting clay

Technique on the wheel

during wedging, and a metal point – a nail, panel pin or needle – with the blunt end buried in a piece of cork (see page 20).

The potter gets the wheel going, quite fast, and wets his hands and the revolving lump of clay from the bowl of water. By applying strong pressure with both hands he will force the clay into a regular revolving solid. 'Is it centred?' is a familiar cry to teachers, for most beginners find the centering process frustrating and are uncertain when it is finished: i.e. when the clay is running true. How true is true? If your hands, when resting on the revolving clay, show any

signs of jiggling about, then it is not running truly enough. There is no need to be tentative when centering and there is no point whatsoever in beginning to shape a hollow pot from a lump of clay which is out of centre, as it will never be any good.

Thus, this tiresome hurdle must be overcome. Brute force is effective. Two robot arms, unflinchingly descending on the wobbling lump would have it centred in a trice, but this is not the only way. By cupping the hands over the clay lump as in the illustration, and alternating the pressure applied by these hands, first more with the left, so the clay rises up in a tower, then more with the right, so it squashes down again like a doorknob, you will effectively bring a wobbly lump of clay into line. It takes several such movements and in the process your hands may become dry. Dip them in water again so that the water can act as a lubricant to prevent the clay under your hands being churned up. Try to remember, though, when removing your hands from the lump in order to wet them or for whatever other reason, to take them off the clay *slowly*. If you take your hands away suddenly, the revolving lump will go off centre again and you will be back where you started.

Often beginners, mesmerised by the wobbling lump, feel that they will never learn this basic centering process and are nonplussed to hear

Use both hands firmly in the centering process, and rest your arms on the wheel surround to steady them.

14

that peasant potters in many lands will throw pots from the top of a large lump of revolving clay without bothering to centre it at all. It is absolutely useless to imagine that you can do the same. When desperation over centering strikes you must remember that the wobbling lump is only clay, soft malleable clay, not a tyrant, and if you concentrate on holding your hands still on the clay while the wheel revolves, the ball underneath *will* become miraculously and seductively smooth. When you have learned by brute force or persuasion to centre the clay perfectly on the wheel, you can be pleased with yourself, since you are now ready to shape the pot.

Drawing up the clay

With the clay running true, make sure you are in a comfortable position – either sitting or standing according to the type of wheel – and with both forearms supported by the edge of the wheel surround (see illustration).

You must make a hollow in the centre of the revolving clay, and many beginners find it easier to press both index fingers or thumbs on the clay towards the centre and downwards. This means you cannot fail to find the centre. Take the fingers away when the hollow is as big as a cherry. Now use your right thumb only in a vertical position (left-handers can carry out this stage with their left thumb, though electric wheels turn anti-clockwise to suit right-handed people) and press it down firmly into the clay like pushing a cork down the neck of a bottle. If you steady your right hand by supporting it with your left, and if you try to keep both forearms pressed against the frame of the wheel, you will be able to do this much more confidently.

Continue to press downwards until you think your thumb is 1cm from the wheel head. This will give you a decent thickness for the base of the pot, and with experience you will be able to reduce the thickness to something more elegant to match your increasing skill. You may find that an airlock holds your thumb in this position, and you must break this by running water over your thumb from a sponge in the other hand. If you

Support your hands when making the hollow.

are making a cylindrical shape, it will need a flat base, and now is the time to make this by pressing the thumb which lies inside the pot away from you, as indicated in the photograph above. Do this steadily and smoothly. Many beginners' pots have untidy, corrugated insides to their bases, and a smooth movement at this stage will not need repeating. Stop when you estimate your thumb is about 1cm from the outside of the clay ball. By now a cross-section of the pot would look like the picture below, and

15

Technique on the wheel

you can draw the wall upwards to the 'inkwell' shape by putting the fingers of the hand on the outside of the pot into use. Use all of the fingers to grasp and squeeze the clay against the pressure of the thumb on the inside, with the wheel still rotating at a fast speed.

Beginners have the habit of allowing the rotation of the wheel and the clay to pull their hands round in the direction of movement. It is best to forget about the fact that the wheel is rotating and simply to pull the hands firmly upwards. The clay will rise up with your hands, for it has nowhere else to go. The natural thing to do is to squeeze the fingers and thumb together, as if grasping and raising a piece of

Drawing up the walls

cloth. If you do this the pot will be short-lived. A twisted ring will come off in your hand and a twisted base will go on revolving below. Set the distance between your fingers and thumb at about 1cm and do not change it. You are aiming to produce a thick-walled cylinder, preferably narrower at the top than at the bottom, with an even thickness of wall. At this stage you must start to use both hands to thin the wall and to increase the height and size of the pot. It is the fingertips of the left hand which are used inside the pot (even if you are left-handed), and the curled index finger of the right hand on the outside. The picture above shows the correct relationship between the hands. Make sure that

both hands are wet with water. If you fail to wet them, the friction with the clay will be too great and your fingers will churn great grooves into the clay wall, which eventually will spiral into disaster. With wet hands positioned as shown in the photograph above, and steadied if possible by resting the elbows on the wheel surround, you can start to draw up the walls of the pot by bringing the hands slightly closer together at their tips, and squeezing the clay between them. The clay must rise upwards, and the wall will ride high above your hands as you raise them together. Keep the wheel rotating at a steady speed – about halfway between stopped and flat-out – and do not increase this speed. By raising your hands up the pot at a steady rate, and keeping them an even distance apart, you will soon learn how much punishment the clay will take, and when it has had enough.

It helps to avoid all jerky movements – especially when your hands first touch or leave the clay. All beginners experience trouble with wobbling and if the embryonic pot is wobbling badly off centre, do not continue. The best course is to scoop the clay off the wheel as the wheel revolves and to centre another piece.

Wobbling can be caused by several things:

1 Clay ball not properly centred.
2 Hollow in the clay not central.
3 Hands drawing up the clay not held steadily.
4 Hands raised too quickly when drawing up the clay.

Wobbling will, of course, be aggravated if you have the wheel going too fast.

It is not possible to teach a beginner entirely with words. Practice is essential, for all instructions are relative and teachers often find they have to give opposite instructions to successive students. 'Make the wheel go faster', 'slow down', 'be firmer with the clay', 'not so rough'. Only a few rules are universal and they relate to the mechanics of the situation. Try and keep these four rules in your mind all the time you are throwing:

1 Never touch the clay with the wheel stopped. You will mess it up.
2 Allow the speed of the wheel to decrease slowly as you get closer to finishing the pot.
3 Keep your hands sufficiently lubricated with clean water – never let them become dry.
4 Always make sure you are doing *something* to the pot. Don't just hold it between your cupped hands as if mesmerised – if you do this the pot will probably soon go off centre.

Shaping

'Now what do I do?' cries the successful beginner who has made a decent cylinder by drawing up the walls three or four times to an even thinness.

You can shape the pot by pressing more with your inside hand to make the pot swell, or narrow it down by pressing more with your outside hand. This latter needs more skill and persuasion, for the clay, like a caged animal, is ready enough to go out, but not so eager to go back. You may need to use both hands,

Aim to make a profile like this

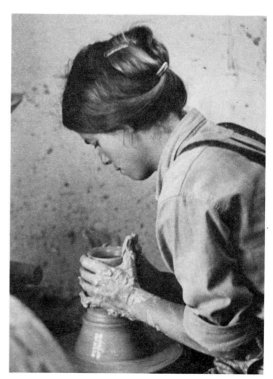

Left and above: collaring the pot with both hands to reduce its width.

the rim outwards, and vice versa. A smoothly finished rim is really important. A piece of damp chamois leather held over the rim will help to give it a perfect, if rather deadened, finish (see

Using the fingers to form the rim

as shown, thumbs facing you, to collar the form inwards, and if you have allowed the top to flare too much, you may not succeed. The ring will flop outwards like an overblown flower and you will have to cut it off as described on page 20.

If you change your straight-sided cylinder into a pot which swells out and then returns to a narrower neck again, you will have done well. If you can produce a nicely finished rim at the top you can be pleased with your efforts. You will use two fingers, one from each hand, to form the rim, and you may find that you get the best results by using the third fingers of each hand. Pressing more with the inside finger will push

Using a chamois leather to smooth a rim.

Making a bowl

Open bowl shapes are not difficult to throw, although beginners often find them rather troublesome, usually because they have the wheel rotating too fast. If you pull a shape with a diameter of 5cm out to a diameter of 10cm, the walls will be rushing through your fingers more than three times as fast, although the wheel is revolving at the same speed. Unless you reduce speed the rim of the bowl will flap about and flop down.

It is the inside profile of the bowl which is immediately in evidence, and it needs to have a smooth curve. Thus the inkwell stage in the drawing-up process can and should be omitted, the base and wall-making movements being combined into one, as indicated in the illustrations below. The bowl can be eased out

Keep hands steady when drawing up the wall.

top picture). Do not try to make the rim too fine. It should reflect the thickness of the pot as a whole, and the tendency of the beginner to make an attenuated and weedy rim is not very satisfactory in itself, and is also misleading about the weight of the pot, as it suggests that it will be light to pick up when very often the opposite is the case.

Do not make the rim too fine; it can easily tear.

to its final form in two or three stages. Do not make it too shallow too quickly, or it may well sit down.

Cutting off the top

The half-made pot with an uneven top can only get worse, as the imbalance of weight of the rotating clay throws it more and more off centre. An uneven rim (often caused by starting with an imperfectly centred ball of clay) must be cut off when it appears, and not left until later. The procedure is simple. With a sharp, fine point mounted on a stick or cork, the revolving pot should be pierced at a level about a centimetre below the unevenness, and with the ease and confidence of a surgeon rather than a murderer.

Do not stab the pot. Rather press the point through from the outside until you can feel it against a finger held on the inside of the pot. Hold it thus for more than one complete revolution and then lift the complete ring of clay from the pot and put it with the waste material. You will now have a newly level rim, and if it is thicker on one side than the other the problem will return as the pot is drawn up again, and you will have to tackle it anew. Uneven tops can be cut off with flexible wire, but beginners are advised to stick to one method – the one that I have just described.

Clay gets tired like most plastic materials, and people too. It should be worked when it is at its

How to cut off an uneven top

fittest. A good plastic throwing clay will become flabby after several minutes' throwing and small vertical cracks will appear where it is under strain – usually where it bulges outwards. The ability to stand up by itself will diminish as the clay is softened with water, and many potters have the disheartening experience of seeing pots which they have coaxed to completion squatting and cracking on the shelf. The lesson – a hard one for the beginner to learn – is to get on with the pot as quickly as possible. When you are satisfied with the shape, don't fiddle around with it, but prepare to cut it off.

Taking a pot off the wheel

The first thing is to make sure that there is a clear space nearby so that you can put the pot down without having to move too much, and preferably without having to get up from the wheel. It is no use thinking about the space when you have the vulnerable, freshly made pot already in your hands. Squeezing a pot in between jars of tools and dangling electric cables is hazardous, and trying to fit pots on to narrow wall shelves often involves squashing the far side irreparably against the wall. Make *plenty* of space for your work before you start. If you can organise a movable flat plank of wood at least 25cm wide, so much the better. This plank, or whatever surface you have cleared, must be clean and not encrusted with dry clay or any lumps to interrupt the passage of the pot when you slide it on.

Trim away surplus clay from the base with a fingernail or a tool before freeing the pot from the wheel head with the cutting wire, as shown right.

A fine twisted brass wire is the best thing you can use to cut the thrown pot from the wheel, although many people today like strong nylon 'trace' as used by fishermen, with a wooden toggle at each end. By revolving the wheel very gently as you pull the wire towards you at the base of the pot, you will ease its work in cutting the pot free. A little water tipped from a cupped hand on to the wheel head on the far side of the pot and pulled through ahead of the wire on a second cut will usually free the pot completely, and as the wire goes underneath, a slight wave disturbance in the base of the pot should be

Technique on the wheel

seen. Too many beginners' pots have either no base at all – so the wire makes an appearance on its way through – or a base built like a fall-out shelter. Learning to make the base just the right thickness takes time.

If you have made a tall pot, do not attempt to lift it from the wheel, rather slide it on to a wet tile or wooden bat held at the same level as the wheel head. Hold the clean wet tile with your left hand and slide the pot with pressure from the first and second fingers of the right hand, pushing the pot near its base. If the pot is reluctant to move, do not force it: run the wire through once more and try again.

The profile of a well-thrown pot

If your pot is bowl-shaped or has a good fat belly, use the first and second fingers of each hand under its belly to lift it up vertically from the wheel. A bowl will sag alarmingly as you do this, but will straighten itself out again when you place it back on a flat surface.

When sliding a freshly-thrown pot on to a tile, make sure that the tile is level with the wheel head so that the progress is smooth. Similarly, moving a large bowl from the wheel to a bat requires smooth, decisive movements.

Very large pots can be difficult to take off the wheel and so can shallow, flaring bowls, thinly thrown. In these cases, potters often put a removable bat on to the wheel head before they start throwing, so that the pot can be removed on a solid surface when it is ready. The adhesive for getting the flat, round wooden bat to stick to the metal wheel head is clay – about the same consistency as throwing clay. It is laid on as a flat pad and grooved or ribbed with a turning tool to provide a vacuum surface when the bat is pressed down on to it. If you jiggle the bat left and right, like testing the steering of a car by moving the steering wheel to and fro, a firm and reliable bond should be made. If not, the forceful process of centering the clay will soon reveal it, and you will have to start again. This very time-consuming process is well worth while for ensuring the success of a very special pot, but the removal of large pots can be assisted with less trouble by putting a patch of sand or grit on to the centre of the wheel head instead of a bat before adding the clay to be thrown. This grit inhibits adhesion at the centre of the base and by shaving away a little of the clay from the foot

By attaching a small sponge to a stick, you can soak up the water from inside a narrow-necked jar before removing it from the wheel.

when the throwing is complete, the adhesion will be so reduced that the pot can be lifted off the wheel with relative ease.

Do not worry too much about thumb-prints on the pot itself. They are ugly if they distort the form, but they are a much more honourable flaw than the unevenness or wobbles which come about when a pot has been handled too tentatively. It is a good idea to run the brass wire or nylon thread under the pot again when it has been taken off the wheel so that it does not bond itself too firmly to its new surface. Pots which have been slid off the wheel on to tiles can become stuck to them like limpets, and this usually results in the cracking of the base and the loss of the pot. However, apart from this final cut, do not touch a freshly made pot with the fingers or any tool when it has just been taken off the wheel. Smoothing down or touching up can be done later if really necessary, when the pot has dried somewhat. Put it out of harm's way, where it will not get nudged by other pots, nor dry too quickly on one side in a patch of

Technique on the wheel

sunlight, or near a warm kiln. Let it dry naturally. On a hot day it will be leather-hard in a few hours. In cold, damp November it may take a week.

Making a lip

Certain shapes are made when the pot is freshly thrown, and the most important of these is the pouring lip of a jug. The illustrations alongside show how it can be done. The key instruction here is to be *firm*. It is extremely difficult to make a pouring lip which pours without dripping. It helps if the edge is really true and thin, and if this is out of character with the pot then make sure that there is at least one sharp edge from which the liquid can run cleanly. It is tiresome, but for once the old dictum, 'what looks right, is right', does not hold good. The most luscious and elegant lips are often bad pourers. It does help if the liquid is channelled towards the lip firmly by

squeezing the flanking wings inwards slightly. This helps to accelerate the flow though it may not prevent a drip running down the front of the jug and on to the table. Unfortunately, the· sharper the edge to the lip or spout, the more likely it is to get chipped or to itself act as a cutting edge, and most potters and tableware

Pouring lips for jugs are made by the opposition of forces: finger and thumb of the left hand pull back while the index finger of the right pulls forwards and downwards; a curving movement then rounds out the shape.
Lips give character and expression to a pot.

manufacturers have to settle for the compromise.

Without becoming involved in the necessary accessories of tableware (lids, handles, etc.), as described in the next chapter, the potter can find throwing a totally absorbing occupation and can make endless variations on vase and bowl shapes which are both elegant and useful. It is essential in this practical book to cover as much ground as possible, and I am reluctant to carry on without allowing the reader to draw breath and consider what beautiful things wheel-thrown pots can be. The pictures on this page and the next show examples of modern thrown ware which I think are good. They are not just examples of throwing – they are thrown, finished and glazed with harmony, each process overlapping with the other and merging so that the results are integrated.

Stoneware bread crock 50 cm high, by Gerry Harvey.

4 Throwing and turning: the finer points

Cider jar and beakers by John Solly, pestle and mortar by Robin Welch, jug by Michael Casson.

The tableware shown here and on the previous pages is thrown, with handles, lids and extras added when the work is leather hard, and the bottoms of the pots neatly finished so that they are even and smooth by the process of turning. The technique of turning is an important one for the beginner to learn, and is explained at the beginning of this chapter. Handles are fun to make and are described in this book both in this chapter and in Chapter 6.

Thrown spouts and lids that fit are the most trying accessories for the beginner to attempt, but for the sake of completeness these, too, are described in this chapter, as simply as possible. The impatient beginner should not linger, however, for everything about the finer points of throwing demands practice – and patience.

Stoneware two-pint jug by Geoffrey Whiting

Turning

Large, upright shapes, jugs, storage jars, if cleanly thrown and carefully lifted from the wheel, need no fussy attention around their bases before they go in the kiln. They are best left to dry out, perhaps running a finger-nail round at the junction of the base and the side, using the same action as a knife scraping a carrot, to chamfer and even out this part of the profile.

On the other hand, shallow shapes, teapots, bowls and any thrown pots requiring a footring, should have their bases modified by 'turning'. In this process the pot is placed upside down on the wheel, and it is the time when many good pots come to grief in inexperienced hands. The potter must choose his moment: when the pot has dried out to a leather-hard state and before the clay has begun to lighten in colour, indicating a brittle state of dryness. If a bowl is placed upside down on a metal wheel head

when it is too soft, its delicate and important rim will be spoilt. If it is too hard it is quite likely to chip. Experience will tell you how leathery the clay should be when it is leather-hard. Perhaps 'cheese-hard' is a better name, for although there are many consistencies of cheese, turning the pot in the right state is quite like paring a firm, rubbery cheese. As with centering the original ball of clay, the upturned pot on the wheel has to be centred again for turning, and the engraved concentric rings on the wheel head are again helpful here. Any pot has to be adequately secured to the wheel before the trimming or turning process begins. You can use water, a long sausage of clay belted around the pot, or a few buttons of clay pressed against the rim, but with all these methods you run the risk of damaging the rim. Many potters, including myself, prefer to place pots not directly on the wheel head but on a pad of harder-than-leather-hard clay flattened on to

Throwing and turning

The photograph and drawings show alternative ways of supporting the leather-hard pot.

Below: turning tools

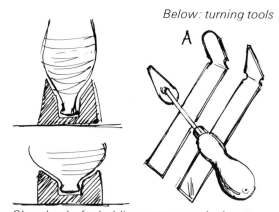

Clay chucks for holding narrow-necked pots.

Use a sharp point or your finger to test for the centre.

the wheel head. The concentric circles can be easily engraved with a sharp point on to this pad as the wheel goes round to help in the positioning of the pot. Tall or top-heavy shapes have to have additional support, as the drawings show.

The turning tool, or any sharp point like a pencil, held against the side of the pot as the wheel revolves, will tell you if you have correctly located your pot in the centre. If the tool you use makes a scratch on one side of the pot only, stop the wheel and push the side with the scratch gently towards the centre of the wheel. Check the pot again for centre by the same method and repeat until you are sure that the pot is turning true.

This may seem a long preamble to the act of turning, but it is important to locate the pot

Clay at the base of the thrown bowl shown on the left gives useful support to the flaring shape. It needs to be carved away in the turning process as shown in the cross-section above.

properly. By so doing you may avoid a lot of painful accidents and the particular chagrin of seeing a decently thrown pot spoilt by this next stage in its making.

The aim of the process is to turn off unwanted clay around the base and often, in the case of a bowl, to make a footring. Shallow bowls need supporting in the throwing with a substantial amount of clay at the base. The picture above right shows how this can be shaved away, reducing the size of the base, giving the walls a consistently even thickness, and the whole pot a fineness and delicacy.

You need a cutting tool which can be held so that the cutting edge is more or less at right-angles to the pot, and popular tools are themselves bent at the end at 90°. The drawing shows the most useful shapes. A curved tool is essential for cutting concave surfaces, and if I were in some way constrained to use but one tool, it would be the one marked 'A'. Hold the tool very near the blade with your right hand and steady its tip against the pot, if you wish, with a finger of your other hand. The cutting edge must be sharp – one often sees students trying to turn pots with tools about as sharp as the average paper knife, which not only makes for hard work but also produces a nasty bumpy surface when the pot is finished. Not many people have a grindstone available nowadays, but most have a metal file, and that is all that is needed to keep a decent edge on the turning tool.

The action of turning is rather like peeling a potato or an apple, except that in the case of pottery it is the potato which is revolving and the knife that is held still. Probably potato-peeling machines mirror the action even more closely. Hold the tool at right-angles and cut away the leathery clay so that it falls in ribbons from the revolving pot. Wheel speed must be moderate and care should be taken to 'enclose' the form with the left hand so that you can catch the pot if it tries to jump off the wheel. Kick-wheels are popular for turning, and it is certainly important to have good control of the wheel at low speeds.

Mark the position of the footring at the base of a bowl before you start carving away the clay. Hold the tool as indicated.

Too much time is spent by students turning the bases of pots. They are usually trying to put to rights a pot with too thick a base, but quite often they will turn right through it or make it wafer-thin so that it cracks or distorts in the kiln. Feeling the base carefully for thickness before putting the pot on the wheel head may help you to assess how much to cut away, and likewise tapping the pot with the sensitive tip of your finger can also give an indication of thickness, but you are sure to go through one or two bases before you get it just right.

Most people regard turning as a corrective process, and in this light the turning should be done swiftly. Others feel that the pot's base must be immaculate and they enjoy the time spent cleaning it up, like dusting under the doormats, in case anyone should look. In fact, potters and others tend to turn pots upside down partly as a reflex action, like looking at the back of an Oriental rug, or the hallmark on a silver spoon, but partly in the hope of the special aesthetic pleasure derived from a handsome piece of turning.

Occasionally pots are cut from the wheel rather crookedly with the wire, condemning them to stand forever slightly askew. Turning is the potter's opportunity to rectify this, and to even up the base. By holding a flat tool or ruler across the

base, he can check for level by making sure that the tool does not wobble as the pot goes round. If it does, let a fine pointed tool like a needle just mark the base in a series of grooves where it is high. These can then be cut away with the turning tool held as shown below, thus levelling the base. At the same time, the base should be made slightly concave, either with a turning tool or by pushing the centre gently down with the fingers. This is a useful insurance policy against the pot's wobbling *after* firing, as the shapes of pots do change inside the kiln and a flat base can become slightly convex under heat, especially if it is supported on a stilt (see Chapter 7). It is thus

Deep grooves made with a sharp point will help the potter to level off a crooked base with a turning tool.

that occasionally we suffer the irritations of spinning dinner plates or wobbly teapots; for the potter who is making his own there is no need for this, and no excuse.

Chatter markings

Ugly undulations appear on the clay if a blunt turning tool is held loosely in the hand or at the wrong angle. Beginners find these 'chatter markings' only seem to get worse if they tighten their grip on the tool and increase pressure. The best remedy is to sharpen the cutting edge of the tool and to change the angle of attack against the pot, so that the tool is neither dragging over the clay surface nor digging into it. If the chatter marking or juddering is very severe it is best to use a sharply pointed tool to incise parallel grooves over the affected area, which then can be more easily turned away.

Handles

A great many pots need handles, and these are attached to thrown pots when leather-hard, but after the turning has been done. They can be made in several ways, and mechanical methods are described in Chapters 6 and 14. For thrown pots, however, the best handles are *pulled*. It is an attractive technique which can be learned without difficulty.

Short carrots of clay should be rolled out from wedged clay which matches the material from which the pots were thrown. With the fat end held in the left hand the carrot is lengthened and smoothed with the other hand, the surface well lubricated with water. It is the space between the thumb and the forefinger when they are squeezed together, not the fingertips, which is used to shape the handle, and this action will give a distinctive and often elegant cross-section to the handle. The essence of making handles this way is a gentle, smooth pull. If you tug at the clay, the shape will be uneven; if you pull too much towards the end you will make the handle weak and weedy at the bottom. Pressure on the clay should be released before you get to the end so that the handle you are making is

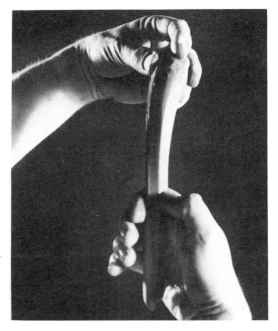

A regular easy movement and plenty of water are needed when pulling handles. Finished handles will arch over naturally when stuck to a board, below.

slightly thicker at both ends, which is how it should be when attached to the pot.

Make more handles than you need, and arch them over, lightly sticking each end down as shown in the photograph. They should not be attached to the pot immediately, but must be put on before the clay stiffens up. It usually takes

If you attach a carrot of clay to the leather-hard pot, the handle can be pulled in situ.

about two hours for the handle to reach the right state of resilience for attaching. When the time comes, shorten the handle to the required length by cutting off each end or breaking the clay away with the thumb and scratch or 'hatch' the two ends with a knife or a pin to provide a roughened area. This should be done very thoroughly, not only to the ends of the handles but to the attachment points on the pot as well, as there is no bond between the handle and pot other than a 'water weld', and the strain on the handle in use can be very great.

The curve of the handle itself, and the way in which both the ends are attached is a matter of taste, but often an amateurish over-large or too small handle can spoil a nicely thrown pot. It is important to compare the prepared handle with the pot by holding them side by side before you commit yourself to joining them for ever. In this regard it is a good idea to have the pot in question in front of you when you are making the handle – this way you do not lose sight of the scale.

Soften the hatched ends of the handle with water or slip, and press the top end against a similarly hatched area on the pot. This should give a good permanent bond, particularly if you wriggle it around a little. The lower end can be attached similarly or simply pressed against a softened spot on the side with thumbs (see picture). If the pot is a big one – anything above the size of a teapot, it is best to pull the handle from a knob of clay already attached to the pot. Such a handle will have a natural look, but like all pulled handles must be well lubricated with water, and many potters carry their pots over to a tap so that the pulling hand can be kept constantly wet.

When both ends of the handle are firmly fixed and the ends smoothed into the contours of the pot with the fingertips or tidied with a modelling tool, it is as well to turn the pot upside down to dry, thus if the handle sags it will have an extra spring and cheerful look when the pot is righted again.

Pulled handles as described above – and as also

Matching jugs thrown by Julia Newman

Teapot by the author

A well-turned pot can be burnished after turning with a wooden modelling tool.

described in Chapters 6 and 14 – can be used on lids, either as straight strips or twisted, or as lugs on the sides of large jars and tureens. Handles can also be made from thrown shapes, to make hoops on top of teapots, and segments of small bowls can be used as lugs on pots such as casseroles. Twisted strips or rolls of clay can also serve the purpose well, although they must all be scratched and softened wherever they join the pot.

Do not let separately made handles dry out too much before you add them to the main pot. They should be flexible, not brittle, when ready, and if too stiff they may even damage the walls of the pot they are added to. The more confident you become, the more easily you will be able to . apply a still-soft handle without over-fingering it.

Casserole by Karen Karnes

Lids

Chapters could be written on lids alone, there are so many varieties, each with its own special qualities. The function of a lid is to seal a pot, although in ceramics the fit can never be an airtight one. If an airtight fit is required, think of corks, or better still, forget about the idea.

Storage jars need lids which are easy to grasp, and they should not be wider than the pot itself or they may get in the way. Coffee pots and teapots must have lids that do not fall out easily, which is why they often have deep throats, to hold them in position.

The illustration shows a variety of thrown lid shapes suitable for different pots. They are not as difficult to make as they look. Starting with a centred lump of clay on the wheel, your fingers will easily and neatly cope with the recesses and flanges as the pictures indicate. Since one cannot make both sides of the lid at the same time, either the top or the under-side must be thrown, and its reverse face turned. The side you choose to throw depends on the shape of the end product. A tall, domed lid is best thrown upside down to minimise the turning (see diagram), whilst a recessed lid can be thrown top-side up since the underneath is almost plain.

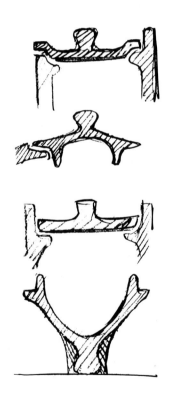

Lids suitable for various kinds of pots. The top one will rest on the top of a storage jar or on a ledge within the form. The bottom drawing shows how a very tall domed lid suitable for a coffee pot is actually made on the wheel upside down.

The stages of making a lid top-side up, and, centre right, throat-side up.

If you have only one pot to 'lid', make two or even three lids immediately after throwing the pot itself, in case one gets broken, and measure the diameter with calipers or a pair of school compasses. If you want several lids for a set of jars, set up a measuring stick beside the wheel as shown on page 40, so the lids come out all the same. Until you are really experienced, make the lids slightly too large – you can always cut them down at the turning stage, but you cannot do anything with a lid which is loose and wobbles.

It is often difficult to crown an elegant thrown body with a lid, so the lid shape should be in your mind when you start on the pot. The best bodies for teapots can look unfinished or dull when unadorned, but come into their own when details are added.

Spouts

Only teapots and coffee pots need spouts, and only those interested in making these pots need the special skills involved. The thrown spout is essentially a tiny, thrown cylinder with a wide, curving base, and it is made with one finger of each hand. Those with large fingers who want to make delicate spouts may substitute a split bamboo stick for the inside finger after the first drawing up. The size of the spout should match the pot (keep the freshly made pot in view when you throw the spout) and the rim of the spout should be fine to help the vessel to pour well. You may want to cut the rim at an angle to improve shape and pouring as shown in the picture below, or you may want to squeeze it when it has dried a little. Punch holes for the tea-leaf strainer in the body of the pot. Slice the base of the spout away, roughen up the new base and the corresponding area on the pot. Attach the spout. Spouts can also be cast by following the instructions in Chapter 6, though combinations of thrown and cast forms are not usually aesthetically pleasing, and if you are casting the spout you might as well cast the body of the pot.

How to make a thrown spout

Teapot by Geoffrey Whiting

Throwing and turning

To make a recess to carry a lid, first flatten the rim with an index finger and then 'split' the rim, as shown right, by pressing downwards with a thumb whilst holding the outside wall steady with the other hand. It is not difficult, though it helps if your thumbnail is fairly short.

Tall vase thrown in two parts by the author

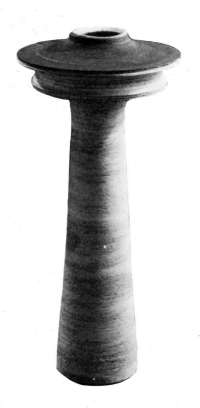

Seals of clay, ribs, flanges, knobs and ears all have a place in a wide spectrum of handmade pottery. If the idea of this sort of decoration appeals, try it out. The pot on the opposite page shows how far this technique can be taken.

Multi-piece pots

Not only handles and spouts can be joined to pots with slip; pots can be joined to one another. Several pieces, thrown separately, can be joined when each piece is leather-hard, and the usual outcome of this is decorative or sculptural pottery. Leather-hard units can be joined on the wheel by roughening and softening the edges that will meet, and the junctions faired-in either with the fingers or a turning tool. Tall, handsome vases can be made in this way – a method which helps in the making of new shapes which would be unstable on the wheel if made in one piece.

If you throw a large pot using as much clay as you can handle, and still want to make it bigger, e.g., as a bread crock or a wine jar, leave a good thick rim on the pot, and leave the pot on the wheel to harden. When it is leather-hard, soften up the rim with hatching and a sponge full of slip, and add a thick ring of similar clay. You can then carry on throwing the pot, fairing the new clay into the walls, with the confidence that the

Right: ornate box with high lid by Ian Godfrey

Throwing and turning

lower part is not going to collapse. This method is very appropriate to adding footrings to the underneath of thrown bowls, as the pictures show.

How to make a thrown footring on a large bowl

If you want to make a set of identical bowls, first weigh out equal-sized balls of clay. When you have made your first master shape, fasten a temporary pointer to the side of the wheel, as shown below, to indicate the position for the bowls' rims.

The practical approach

'What heavy milk you have', said a tactless guest, lifting the hand-made milk jug. However 'right' a practical pot *looks* it is 'wrong' if it feels wrong in the hand. It should feel neither too heavy nor too light for its looks, but it is not only a question of weight. The most elegant cup and saucer is a failure if a spoon will not lie easily in the saucer, or slides into the middle under the cup as soon as the cup is lifted. A coffee pot with a lid that falls out when it is tilted because its centre of gravity is too high, or a teapot with a spout set so gracefully low that tea flows out of the spout whilst it is still being filled from a kettle, will teach you lessons that will not need repeating.

When you are making pots for the house, think about essential practical criteria when planning the pot in your mind. A soup tureen needs an inside profile which matches the soup ladle. A candelabrum needs somewhere to catch the wax that might run down. Work, too, within your capabilities. You could make dozens of matching coffee mugs whilst struggling to make a single teaset. Remember, too, that a drinking vessel is going to have an edge which comes into contact with your mouth, and needs to *feel* nice as well as to look good.

A thoughtful study of function before you start will help you design a shape. Take a casserole as a case study. It needs to be sturdy enough to withstand thermal shock, and to conserve heat well. It must have a lid with a knob you can grasp, though not so high as to foul the oven shelf above. It needs smooth curves inside for easy cleaning, and a pair of handles or lugs on the side coarse enough to be manageable through clumsy oven gloves. It should be wide at the base and wide at the top, it should be the right size for the family it has to serve, which means almost certainly larger than you think when you are making it. When it is glazed, however much you may like a matt or granular surface, it must be shiny for easy and hygienic cleaning.

A traditional charcoal cooking stove has a body thrown in one piece with handles added so that it can be moved easily when hot. Inside the bowl lies a thrown disc with perforations on which the charcoal rests. Air from below is drawn through the triangular hole, and cooking is done on the top. Such a stove must be made from refractory clay.

*Press-moulded dish
by Jean-Claude de Crousaz*

5   Pottery from moulds

*Having explored the possibilities of the
plasticity of clay on the wheel, we can now make
use of the other great property of clay – its
capacity to take and retain an impression. Press
plastic clay against a coin and it will retain a
negative impression of great precision. The
same coin or mould can be used again and
again, making innumerable identical
impressions. If very liquid clay is poured over
the coin and allowed to dry, a similar negative*

*impression or cast will be formed, probably
showing even more detail.*

*For the beginner the use of liquid clay is a little
more difficult. Called 'slip-casting', it is
described in Chapter 6. The present chapter is
concerned with the making of moulds out of
plaster of Paris, and casting from these moulds
dishes and simple shapes, using plastic clay.
This technique is known as press-moulding and
is very easy.*

Introduction

Although practically everyone handles moulded artefacts all day long – from telephones to milk bottles – only specialists are in touch with the moulding process. Most of us have memories of the bucket-and-spade joys of making precise and perfect identical casts. Wet sand has a long and diverse history as a casting medium, in ceramics as well as metal casting, but it is best left to experts. In this book we shall stick to the commonest moulding medium – plaster of Paris.

Plaster of Paris shares certain qualities with clay – it retains an impression, and when it sets, just like fired clay, it is non-deformable and absorbent. It only replaced fired clay as the material of moulds in the last century, and many studio potters still prefer to use fired clay moulds – biscuit moulds – for press-moulding.

The technique is to press sheets of plastic clay against the mould's surface so that the clay picks up the form of the mould, and to leave it until it has hardened, when it can be removed and finished or fettled ready for the kiln.

The limitation of press-moulding is one of shape – it is not possible to remove from the mould, whether it is convex or concave, a three-dimensional form which turns back on itself, as the diagrams show. The most popular shapes for press-moulds are shallow dishes. Universally useful on the table, especially if they are oval, they are easy to make if they have gently sloping sides.

Clay packed around a three-dimensional shape makes a precise record of that shape, and in this way ancient clays have provided us with the only record we have of some fossil forms. The clay mould shown here illustrates how clearly details are recorded and such details can be made permanent if the clay mould is fired in the kiln.

Mouids have to be made from a 'master' shape, which can be a ready-made object such as an upturned polythene bowl, or even a sea-shell or a fossil, but most potters prefer to make their own masters from solid clay.

Provided they are not too big, solid circular forms can be made on the wheel by a combination of throwing and turning using hardish plastic clay which should be well-finished with a chamois leather or wooden tool to give a smooth surface. Masters for oval dishes and platters are made by hand on a flat tabletop following a shape which should be drawn out on card placed below the intended

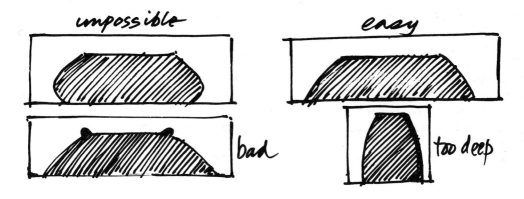

impossible *easy*

bad *too deep*

Pottery from moulds

form. Irregular shapes are popular because the masters are easier to make, but the results are often boring. Non-circular symmetrical shapes such as ellipses are better and worth the effort. Time spent smoothing down a clay model will be rewarded, for the moulds show up any irregularity in the original and by then it is too late to do anything about it. Remember to make the master shape flat on the top, otherwise the finished pot will rock about or need 'legs' for support, and check its symmetry by using a cardboard template.

When you are quite satisfied with the shape, make sure that the surrounding area is clear and clean and level. You must surround the model with a wall of clay, wood or linoleum called a 'cottle', standing a few inches away from, and a few inches higher, than the master.

Liquid plaster is about as heavy as golden syrup, and can make about as much of a mess. It is essential when pouring plaster over a form to contain the liquid within a strong wall. It is amazing how many students who have taken ages over their model will skimp on the frame or cottle, and then be horrified to see plaster overflowing on to tools and wrist watches on the bench and spilling over shoes on the floor. It is simple to strengthen the wooden or linoleum surround to the clay form by building up substantial clay supports on the outside.

Make a strong wall around the clay shape before pouring in the plaster.

Remember the principles of dam building and make this wall thick at the bottom. Plaster suitable for mould-making is generally sold as superfine dental or surgical plaster and it is white. Do not use the pink, gritty variety used on house walls, as this is too coarse and does not give enough detail. Apart from ceramic suppliers (see page 133) the source of superfine plaster is the chemist's shop.

Make sure that the plaster you use is fresh. Storing plaster away for years is worse than storing garden seeds. It becomes 'slaked' and will not harden properly. Moulds made from such plaster will crumble and chip and any casts they yield will have very little sharpness of detail. For this reason it is best to buy plaster in fairly small quantities – three to ten kilos at a time rather than in huge bags.

Mixing plaster

When you are mixing plaster, roll up your sleeves. Put clean, cold water into a plastic bowl, but do not fill it more than half full. Have the plaster in a plastic bin near at hand, not halfway across the studio, and *using one hand only* sprinkle it, handfuls at a time, into the water as one would 'dredge' sugar or flour. Do this from a height of about 30cm above the water – this will mean that the plaster is likely to reach the water in a fine shower and not in lumps. The water will eagerly swallow up the first few handfuls. Carry on adding plaster in handfuls until the small white island of plaster projects from the middle of the white lake in the bowl. I find it always takes rather more handfuls of plaster than one expects. Now is the time to use the other hand to stir the plaster, breaking down any lumps between the fingers. It is essential to use your hand for this – a tool is not sensitive enough – and it is very important for even strength in the mould to get rid of all the lumps. By keeping your plaster-supplying hand dry, you can if necessary add another handful of plaster if the mixture seems very watery. The consistency of single cream will become like double cream in about three minutes, and you must be ready to pour the plaster around the model before it becomes viscous and sluggish.

Sprinkle plaster in handfuls into the bowl until it no longer sinks below the surface.

Before pouring, wash both your hands and remember that any plaster which comes off them will contaminate the clay store or the settling tank, or block the drains.

It will take about ten minutes for freshly made plaster to harden up; during this time it will become quite warm to the touch. This heat is given off during the chemical process by which water is re-absorbed into the interlocking crystal bundles of the solid calcium sulphate. It is an exothermic reaction, the reverse of the process by which the plaster of Paris is made in the first place, when heat is applied in order to free chemically combined water from the calcium sulphate mineral.

As soon as the plaster has set, strip away the surrounding wall and nudge the mould free from the tabletop. You should pull out the clay master without delay and wash the newly revealed mould clean with soapy water. Examine the mould carefully for pin-holes caused by air bubbles. Pin-holes will make mole-like blemishes on subsequent casts and should be filled up – the best filler being clay.

The mould should be left to dry for a day or so

before use. It will 'sweat' for some time, and if dried too fiercely becomes rather brittle.

Leather-hard clay pressed into these hollow moulds will have an outside shape which matches the original master, now destroyed, but the inside profile depends upon your skill. A slab of clay rolled flat with the rolling pin between guide bars, as shown, can be lowered carefully into the mould while it is still flexible, and pressed gently into position. By using a shaped piece of hard rubber, known to potters as a 'rubber kidney', or an equivalent bendy, curved form, you can scrape the inside surface smooth without leaving fingerprints, and you should use a sharp knife to cut the top level with the mould before the clay becomes too dry. The rim should be given careful attention. If you cut unevenly the dish will look clumsy.

Clay of even thickness can be laid into moulds when it is still flexible but not floppy.

Pottery from moulds

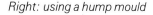

Use a rubber kidney and a little water to smooth the inner surface of the press-moulded dish.

Right: using a hump mould

Press-moulded dishes should not be removed from the moulds until they have hardened up considerably. If they can dry out inside the moulds they stand less chance of warping – a problem which is commonly caused by the use of clay of uneven thickness.

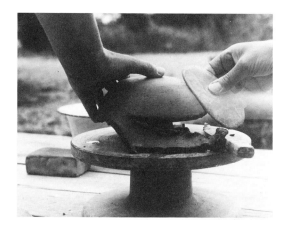

Shallow and open forms always show off their insides, and press-moulded dishes offer a particularly good opportunity for decoration by slip-trailing or painting (see Chapter 16). Patterns can be inlaid into press-moulded dishes, and this is most successful when using convex or hump moulds, so that the pattern appears on the inside of the dish. Hump moulds are made by pouring plaster into a prepared hollow, and an existing press-mould as just described can be used for this. However, plaster sticks to plaster unless a separator is put on to the surfaces, and the most handy separator is very watery slip, brushed or sponged thinly over the surface. Soft soap or warm Vaseline or olive-oil, or a mixture of these will do equally well. Hump moulds are usually made with stalks like mushrooms so that they can be more easily

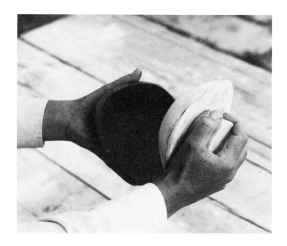

handled. The stalk is added by scoring the surface of the drying plaster, building a small circular clay wall round the central area and pouring in a second small mix of plaster.

The convex shape you have now made should be prized away from the hollow mould or whatever other concave subject you have used, and the clay or other separator washed from the surfaces. The hump mould can then be used to make dishes from sheets of clay as shown left.

Footrings can easily be added to the bases of pots made on hump moulds, either by the use of a coil or a small, thrown ring (see the picture on page 83). Small patterns of contrasting plastic clay can be pressed on to the surface before the clay sheet is overlaid, and an inlaid design is the result, as described in Chapter 16.

Once you have made your mould you can make a great many identical dishes from it until your friends and relations simply do not know what to do with them. The clay, the colour, and the patterns can vary, but the basic shape will not, unless you carve or sculpture the rim or press into the mould a sheet of clay which itself has already been carved, as shown in the picture below.

A natural form like a leaf or half an orange can be used as the basis of a mould provided the shape does not turn back on itself.

Keep your moulds tidily in a dry place away from your working area. If they are piled up in a heap they are likely to damage one another, and it is best to put them face to face in a cupboard, to keep the dust out.

It is a good idea to chamfer off the outside corners of the moulds so that they have smooth edges. In this way they will not damage one another so easily, nor will they shed plaster into precious clay.

Fantasy ceramist Alan Barrett-Danes made a mould of a cabbage leaf by pouring plaster over the convex leaf itself. The resulting casts made by pressing plastic clay against the mould could

Press-moulded form by Jane Waller

Pottery from moulds

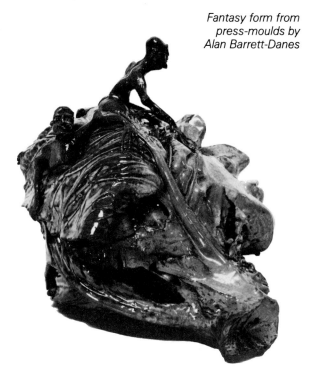

Fantasy form from press-moulds by Alan Barrett-Danes

be bent and folded into extremely realistic recreations of the cabbage for his own sculptural purposes.

Be inventive

By inserting a flexible object between a hump mould and the sheet of clay (say a coarse-textured old dishcloth), the inside of the bowl can take a second impression. This decoration, left when the dishcloth is removed, can be emphasised if filled with contrasting slip (see Chapter 16).

Think of a mould as the tool, not as an end in itself. There are so many imaginative ways in which the clay's willingness to take an impression can be used. Moulded shapes can be used in conjunction with pinching (see Chapter 10), coiling (Chapter 11), and slab-building (Chapter 12), as well as combined clay techniques (Chapter 13).

The pattern created by coarse cloth can be used as the basis for an inlaid design of slip.

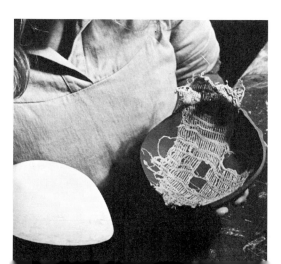

6 Slip-casting

Slip-casting can open a completely new world to both the adventurous and the hesitant potter. It offers the opportunity of making complicated and bizarre forms to the one, and a high degree of precision in finish to the other. Best of all, it is very economical of equipment and expense. Like pinched pottery it has made great strides in art schools in the last decade and is ideally suited to small-scale operations at home.

It is probably because the technique is primarily used for producing identical pots in vast numbers that it has until recently been ignored by the craft potter, and because there is always so much to learn in an evening class or pottery course, it is often neglected here too. This is not because it is especially hard, but rather because it cuts across all other processes by being different. Like press-moulding, described in the previous chapter, it relies on plaster of Paris forms, but unlike all the other techniques described in this book it uses clay in a non-plastic state – as a liquid – and the techniques of rubber or plastic injection-moulding are more useful as analogies.

If liquid slip is run into a hollow mould, some of it will harden against the side, and if the surplus is poured away, a thin skin will be left, copying the mould in every detail. The clay must be liquid enough to flow absolutely evenly, but not so watery that it shrinks and cracks when it dries. Slip is clay and water; casting slip is clay and water with the addition of deflocculents. A correctly prepared casting slip has the advantages of liquidity without the disadvantages of shrinking.

By adding a small proportion of sodium silicate or 'waterglass' and sodium carbonate or 'soda ash' to a thick and creamy slip, it will become much more runny.

These magical thinners, sodium silicate and sodium carbonate, are usually bought as a sticky syrup and sugar-like crystals respectively. They are used in approximately equal and very small quantities to make a thick viscous slip as runny as motor oil. They are deflocculents, which act chemically on the clay molecules like a breath of air on a house of cards. Most ceramic

Slip-casting

suppliers have their own recipes for making casting slip from powdered ingredients, and give detailed instructions for their preparation. The beginner would do well to buy such a casting slip kit and follow the instructions carefully, or buy a liquid slip ready prepared. However, it is an interesting experience to make your own, and two recipes are given below:

Stoneware casting slip

Powdered clay (Moira pale stoneware)	5 kg
Water	1 litre
Soda ash	10 g
Sodium silicate	7.5 g
Total weight	1750 g/litre

Porcelain casting slip

Ball clay	300 g
China clay	2200 g
Felspar (potash)	1250 g
Flint	1250 g
Water	2.2 litres
Soda ash	13 g
Sodium silicate	13 g
Total weight	1800 g/litre

Mixing casting slip

The best way to make the slip is to mix the two deflocculents together and dissolve them in half a cupful of warm water. Add most of this to the measured quantity of water given above and mix it thoroughly with the powdered ingredients, making sure that there are no lumps which will take a long time to soften up. The mixture will be unfamiliarly syrupy and will trickle off your hand like thin glue. It must then be passed through an 80 or 100 mesh lawn, using a plastic scrubbing brush, into a plastic bowl or bucket. Into this receptacle the slip will fall in semi-solid clots – a thixotropic gel. Give it a stir with a wooden stick and, magic, it will be liquid again. Do not beat it up like whipping cream, for air bubbles in slip cause trouble in the cast.

Fine-mesh phosphor bronze lawn for sieving slip

The slip needs passing through a lawn several times to make sure it is smooth. Plunge your hand into the bucket. If the slip runs off your fingers in fine rivulets it is probably the right consistency (see facing page). If it is sluggish, add the remaining deflocculent bit by bit. It is best to be sparing with the deflocculent and to add only what you need to achieve the engine-oil consistency I have mentioned. If you add too much the process will go into reverse and the slip will coagulate into slippery lumps like piles of jellyfish and in this form it cannot be used. If you have the misfortune to find your slip in this state, the best thing to do is to add more clay and water in the same proportions as in the recipe until the deflocculent balance is achieved again. Let a prepared casting slip stand overnight before use.

Your aim is to achieve as heavy or dense a slip as possible – at least 1750 grams to the litre. Density will increase if you leave the lid off the container so that the water evaporates, but fluidity may also be lost, and if you always keep a lid on the casting slip container you will keep powdered clay, plaster of Paris and other foreign bodies out of it. Smoothness is absolutely essential if the cast is to be an elegant one. Although slip will keep for months once it is made, it has to be sieved every time it is used.

Slip-casting

Try your slip first in a simple, clean, dry plaster mould such as used for the moulded work described in Chapter 5. Pour freshly sieved slip from a large plastic jug until it fills the mould to the very top, with a healthy reverse meniscus standing proud over the rim. Be ready to top this up with more after a few minutes, as the level falls with the absorption of water by the plaster walls. A crust of clay will dry against the side, and only with experience will you learn how long to wait before pouring out the liquid slip in order to leave a cast of appropriate thickness. It depends on several factors, not least the state of the plaster mould, which will be less absorbent after each successive cast. Normally five to ten minutes is adequate and the liquid contents of the mould should then be returned to the slip

After sieving the syrupy casting slip, its fluidity can be restored by stirring.

Slip-casting

mould dry out like a wet pavement in the sunshine.

Leave the cast in the mould for a further hour or two and then turn it out gently on to your hand. If your casting slips have been correctly prepared, it will be firm and leathery. If it is flabby, and bends in at the edges, you have probably taken it out of the mould too soon, or perhaps used too much deflocculent in the slip. If it takes too long to dry, there is too much water in the slip; if it cracks, the mould has been used too dry.

bucket by lifting up the mould and pouring out the surplus in a single, smooth movement. Resist the temptation to shake it or tap on the mould – this will only cause unevenness in the cast, and try to hold the cast upside down for as long as you can, so that all the still-liquid slip can run out. If the mould is turned upright again too soon, the slip will pool awkwardly in the bottom. After a few minutes, run a sharp knife around the edge of the cast as shown below to give the form a clear, even rim. Soon you will have the pleasure of seeing the glossy slip inside the

The level of slip in a mould may need topping up as it loses moisture to the plaster. How long the casting slip is left in the mould depends on the dryness of the mould and the character of the slip. The thickness of the clay drying around on the rim gives you a clue. Soon after emptying the surplus slip from the mould you can clean up the edge with a knife.

It is customary to let a mould 'rest' for an hour or two before refilling with slip, and if you want to get an impressive production rate then have several moulds on the go at the same time. The drawings on the top of the next page show the

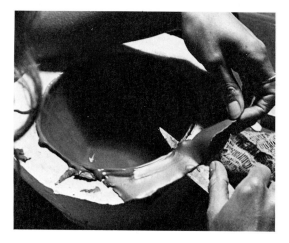

Suitable shapes for one-piece moulds

various shapes which can be conveniently slip-cast from the single-piece mould – deeper and more complicated shapes than one would attempt with the press-moulding technique.

Unfortunately, when a cast is bone-dry and ready for fettling before firing, it is extremely brittle and only shapes which are inherently strong, such as spheres, can be handled with confidence. Shallow bowls and plates are as brittle as poppadoms, and at this stage must be handled with the greatest care. Only experience will tell you the lightness of touch needed to hold such a cast, but on the other hand the processes of adding handles and joining casts together is swift and un-messy. Simply dip the handle ends lightly into the slip and place them gently on the side of the cast. No wriggling about is necessary as with leather-hard pots made with plastic clay. The damp spots suck the

components together in a clean join that needs no fettling. Do not be tempted to touch up the joints with a modelling tool – the pristine surface of the cast will be destroyed.

It is as well to practise with one-piece moulds but, as explained in Chapter 5, the forms are limited to shapes which can be pulled away from the mould, and can have no undercut edges. What slip-casting offers is the possibility of making complicated enclosed forms which could not be thrown or modelled, using multi-piece moulds which are assembled, filled with slip and later taken apart piece by piece to yield the finished shape inside. Now the reason why one needs to control and limit shrinkage in the slip immediately becomes clear – a complete teapot inside a multi-piece mould would simply crack to bits as it dries under the constraint of the plaster walls.

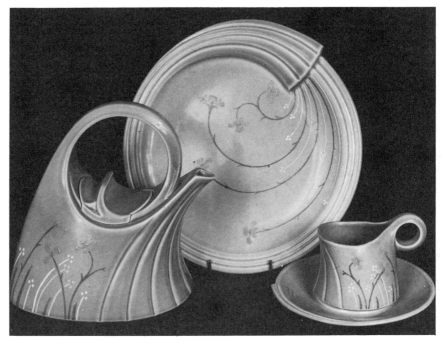

Slip-cast teaset by Rosemary Fiona Talbot

A complicated form may need a dozen pieces carefully assembled for each cast, and this, the domain of the fine china factories, is well out of the scope of this book. But there is no reason why the beginner should not learn to slip-cast, from a two-piece mould, a finished object in the round.

Squashed toothpaste tubes or gymshoes can be used as casting 'masters', but for practical domestic ware we can take as our subject a coffee mug complete with handle. Design the mug carefully and throw a thick cylinder with walls about 1cm, using hardish clay. Allow it to harden slightly and then with a turning tool shape the *outside* to the form of a practical but oversized coffee mug, leaving a high extra rim as indicated alongside. When this has become leather-hard, invert it on the wheel and turn the base so that it is level and smooth. Make sure you use very fine-textured, ungrogged clay for making the master. Put on an even-section handle, preferably made by the simple method, as shown opposite. Drag a looped wire through a bar of clay, bend the strip of clay which comes out of it into shape, cut it to length, and when

Slip-cast apples in an acrylic box by Roger Honey

appropriately firm, attach it to the coffee mug as neatly as you can, so that the handle abuts to the pot rather than seeming to grow out of it. Make sure the surface of the mug is as smooth and

A wooden turning tool helps to form the extra high rim on the coffee mug master.

54

unblemished as possible and fire the pot, with its extra top rim, to the biscuit state when it is dry. You must now fill the inside of the pot with plastic clay, and embed the pot *on its side* in a pad of stiffish plastic clay with the handle horizontal, as if it were floating in a clay bath. The clay must come exactly halfway up the pot and the junction of the clay bed with the pot must be clean. Paint over the exposed parts of the biscuit pot carefully with thin clay or warm Vaseline, and then press three small balls of clay, not much larger than garden peas, on to the clay surround. Cut the clay 'bath' to a square plan, a minimum of 3cm away from the master except at the top of the mug, where the cut must coincide with the top of the high rim of the master (see the drawing below right). Make a cottle from four pieces of wood (see drawing on page 57), strengthen with clay buttresses and pour the plaster, ensuring that it rises at least 3cm above the biscuit mug. This will become mould A.

Attaching the handle to the master

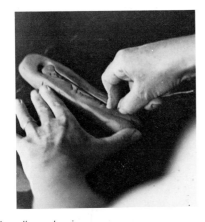

A wire loop handle-maker in use

When the plaster has dried, remove the cottle and turn the block upside down so that the plaster of mould A is on the tabletop, and carefully pull away the clay from the biscuit pot and the new mould, making sure that the biscuit pot stays in place. The three garden peas of clay will have left indentations in the mould and the entire exposed surface will be rather sticky with clay. Make sure there is a film of clay to act as a separator for the next mould, but remove any lumps or blobs of clay that would otherwise spoil the surface. Replace the cottle, very carefully sealing its fit with the plaster block with clay, and add two very fine worms of clay leading from the handle to the cottle wall at the positions marked X and Y. These will act as blow-holes for the casting slip later, to ensure that the handle is perfectly and properly cast. Pour a new mix of plaster over the model and let it dry. This will become mould B. When it has

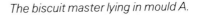

The biscuit master lying in mould A.

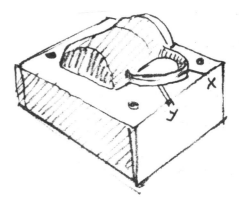

Slip-casting

The separate parts of a two-piece mould must be held together with rubber bands when slip-casting.

hardened, strip off the cottle and very gently ease the plaster moulds apart at the junction, which will show as a grey clayey line.

Your original biscuited master should come out intact, and you can clean up the moulds ready for use. The 'garden peas' will now have made male and female keys for helping you to re-position the mould accurately, and the two thin worms of clay will have left fine tubes leading from the handle to the outside. When the moulds have sweated for a day or two, you can start casting in them, although the first cast is not normally a very satisfactory one.

Bind the two moulds A and B together with two large rubber bands cut from an old inner tube of a car tyre – most people have one in their garage, and if you do not, your neighbour will. Make sure the two moulds are a really tight fit – if necessary, put pencils or blocks of wood down inside the rubber bands to make them tighter. You can now fill the mould through the opening at the top, and soon the function of the extra rim on the biscuited mug will become clear. It is what the ceramics industry calls a 'spare' – it simply means a spare and extra piece of casting which can be broken off or cut away when the casting is complete, thus protecting the rim of the pot itself and ensuring an even thickness. The gradual lowering of the level of slip down the spare as the walls of the mould take up the plaster can clearly be seen, and it is a good idea to top-up the slip, although the use of the spare makes this no longer essential. When the slip has been poured out after ten minutes or so, and the cast is drying, the clay in the spare can be pared away, or it can be cut off when the cast is released from the mould, as shown. Our coffee mug will fall out of its moulds complete with handle, which will be a solid handle if the cast is a reasonable thickness. Too thin a cast will result in a hollow handle, which is both impractical and ugly.

The resulting casts should be fettled to a fine degree of finish with a sharp knife, and very fine sandpaper can be used to remove the 'rib' where the two moulds join.

Separate the press-mould carefully. The still-rubbery coffee mug will soon be ready for fettling.

The mould you have made can be used to turn out from 20 to 50 casts. The alkali in the casting slip attacks the plaster, which will not produce a clear form for ever, but at least it gives you the opportunity of making an unusual form in identical units, and in many cases (though not in the case of our coffee mug) the opportunity of making a form which you would not be able to make in any other way.

Tableware slip-cast by Ruth Duckworth

Other domestic pots which can be sensibly cast are salt and pepper pots, often too small to throw easily, and square, or squarish, storage jars. It is worth designing moulds for vessels which cannot easily be made on the wheel, and which are required in identical units. The casting technique can also be used for decorative and sculptured pots, modelled figures and in conjunction with the techniques described in Section Two of the book.

7 Glazing: principle and technique

The process of glazing simply means putting on to the surface of the pot, usually after the pot has been fired to a porous or 'biscuit' state, the mixture of those ingredients which, when heated up to vitrification temperature, will form a glassy and permanent coating on the finished pot. It is capable of infinite variation, both in the technique of application and in the nature of the finished result. The glaze may well contain many of the elements of decoration (see Chapters 9 and 16), certainly those of colour and texture, either within itself or by the way in which it is applied.

It would not help the beginner to pretend that it is easy or that there are any short cuts to success. For many, glazing is the most difficult part of pottery making. It is not necessary: pots can be left 'finished' in the porous, once-fired state, though such pots are dust catchers and impractical for storing food or liquids. For many potters, however, especially those more interested in colour and pattern than in form, glazing is the most exciting part, which lifts their ordinary pottery into the realms of the extraordinary.

It is important to note that certain kinds of pottery are best served by certain types of glaze and the specialists who have contributed chapters on slab-building, pinching and raku have indicated in these chapters glaze recipes appropriate to their products. In the present chapter we are concerned only with the method of application. Glaze recipes for domestic ware are given in the next chapter.

Salt and soda glazes

From medieval times, both decorative and functional ware has been glazed by introducing common salt (sodium chloride) or soda ash (washing soda) into the kiln packed with pots, when the temperature is at about 1100°C. The crystals volatilise and deposit droplets of melt on to all surfaces within the kiln, just as water vapour condenses onto glass or the walls of a steamy bathroom. It is an easy method, but because the salt is so volatile at high temperatures, it is indiscriminate, and the kiln,

once used in this way, will go on coating its contents with salt (greeny-grey) or soda (coral-pink) every time it is heated up. An electric kiln cannot be used for salt glazing as the elements are damaged by the deposit, and such glazing must always be done in an outdoor kiln because of the noxious fumes.

Salt-glazed pots have a mottled appearance, like orange-peel, and often the coating is uneven. The pot in the picture above shows it well, and stoneware drainpipes, often beautifully coloured with salt glaze, are familiar to most people.

The potassium in wood produces its own fluxing effect. Where pots are in direct contact with sticks or organic matter in a wood-fired kiln they gain an irregular coating of glaze at very

Random ash glaze from a wood-fired kiln on a pot by Janet Leach

Glazing

high temperatures when the potash joins forces with the alumina and silica in the pot body. The more normal method of using wood ash, however, is in the much more common water-mixed glazes.

Water-mixed glazes

Most potters apply glaze to biscuit pots by mixing dry ingredients with water, spraying or pouring this on to the pots, or dipping the pots into it. The water will be absorbed by the porous clay body of the pot and on the surface will be left a film of powder which quickly dries. From that time until it is fired in the kiln the pot is very vulnerable to damage, as the glaze has no more adhesive power than flour on the surface of pastry.

The thickness of the glaze coat left on the pot is important, as it affects the colour (most glazes are rather darker when they are thin and lighter when they are thick) and is controlled partly by the consistency of the glaze in the bucket. The old rule 'thicker than milk, thinner than cream' is a good general guide, especially as glaze mixed up in a bucket often looks like cream in a pail.

If the pot to be glazed is very porous, or is warm, it will absorb more water, and consequently a thicker coat of glaze will be left on the surface. Similarly, if the pot is dipped into a bucket of glaze for a long time, or is sprayed at length, a thicker layer will accumulate.

The ceramic suppliers listed on page 133 all offer earthenware and stoneware glazes with individual characteristics to studio potters, and the beginner may want to choose these ready-prepared glazes. They at least remove some of the anxiety from glaze-making, even if a good deal of the excitement is lost at the same time. If you have the inclination to experiment with your own glazes, you will find some recipes in Chapters 8 to 12.

Whether you buy your glaze ready-mixed as a powder in a bag, or weigh out the powdered ingredients of your own recipe, preparing the glaze will be done in the same way. A sensible

Ingredients weighed dry are put together in a bowl before adding water.

usable quantity to mix is 3 kg. Put the dry materials in a polythene bowl, and check with your fingers for any hard lumps, crushing any you can find. Then add about 4 litres of water (the amount is not critical), stirring the mix with a wooden spoon or your fingers. Cautious potters will wear rubber gloves and even a face mask to protect themselves from dust particles. When the mixture has become an even-textured cream, put it all through a fine sieve – a phosphor bronze 'lawn', as used for sieving slip,

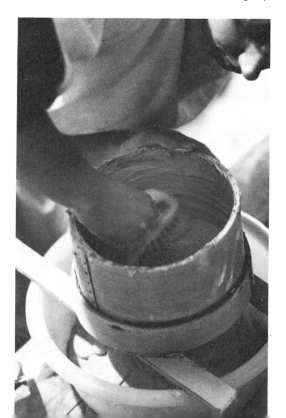

into another polythene bowl or bucket. Your glaze is sticky, clayey stuff, and will not go through easily. You may need a scrubbing brush to help you. Choose a plastic one, with white bristles, as these are the easiest to keep clean. Do *not* use your finger nails to rub the glaze through the sieve, as the untarnishable mesh is stronger than they are, and will soon wear them down to the quick. The glaze should be put through the lawn more than once, and the potter must make sure that *everything* goes through. Any stubborn matter left in the lawn will mean that the glaze in the bucket will not have the composition you planned.

When sieving glaze make sure that everything goes into the bowl, or the mixture may be wrong.

Glaze, once mixed, should be stored in a wide mouthed jar or a polythene bucket with a lid, and in time the heavy ingredients will fall to the bottom. To overcome this some potters add bentonite, a form of clay with the properties of holding the glaze ingredients in suspension. A proportion of 2½ per cent of the total weight will do the trick without changing the nature of the glaze itself.

The method you use for getting the glaze evenly on to the pot depends partly on the shape of the pot: tall thin pots are easy to glaze by dipping the entire thing in the glaze bucket, but wide flaring bowls and bulging pots with narrow necks are not so easy, and very large and intricate forms pose special problems.

Spraying

A spray gun is no longer a rarity in studio potteries, but it does require a fair amount of expensive back-up equipment. The gun itself, like a paint sprayer, needs a reservoir for the glaze and a pressure of about 2.5 kg/sq cm from an air compressor. It is directed at the pot on a turnable which is slowly rotated, and placed at the entrance to a spraying booth. This essential booth can be as simple as a large cardboard box, but a metal booth with an extractor fan is best, and vital in a workshop where a lot of people will be breathing the air.

Apart from the cost of the equipment, spraying has other disadvantages: much of the glaze will fly past the pot and be wasted; it is difficult to give a coat of even thickness all over the surface; and the glaze has to be sieved regularly, to prevent the spray gun from blocking up. It is all too easy to glaze pots too thickly on their shoulders, and not at all under projecting flanges. At the same time the technique suits certain types of pots, particularly slip-cast ware, which retains its 'untouched by hand' appearance, and an important advantage of spraying is that it avoids finger marks.

The insides of narrow-necked vessels cannot be glazed with a spray gun, and such pots have to be filled with glaze from a jug as described below to glaze their inner surfaces.

Dipping and pouring
Glazing the inside

The inside surface of a pot, whether it is a bowl or a tall jar, is usually glazed before the outside. Glaze is poured into the pot from a jug, usually almost to the top, and then poured swiftly out again with a turning movement of the wrist to make sure that all the internal surface is covered. The glaze has to be rolled around the inside of a large bowl, and then poured out

Glazing

Glaze poured into a vessel (above) is poured out again straight away (below), twisting the pot around so that all the inside is covered.

neatly to prevent drips running down the outside. Do not hesitate; a porous biscuit pot will voraciously drink up water from the glaze, and leaving a glaze standing inside a pot for five seconds can make the coat of glaze too thick. It will also mean that the wall of the pot has absorbed a good deal of moisture, and will therefore be less ready to soak up more when glaze is put on the outside. This is important, for a thinner coat of glaze adhering to the outside of the pot will mean a difference in the quality of the glaze, often an unhappy variation in the final appearance of the pot. It is wise to wait at least

half an hour before glazing the outside, and much more if damp patches appear through the clay wall. The pot must be completely dry on the outside before you carry on.

Glazing the outside

A cylindrical-shaped pot is glazed on the outside by plunging it vertically into the glaze bucket, holding the pot by its base, up to the point where your fingers are gripping it. Withdraw the pot after a second or two, giving it a twist to fling off

Pouring the outside of a small bowl

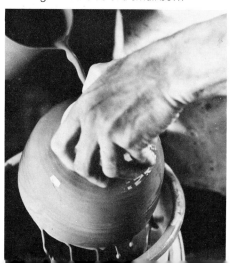

any droplets of glaze from around the rim. The pot should now have an even coat all over, except for the final centimetre on the outside, and the base. Since a stoneware pot has to be kept clean of glaze on its base anyway, to prevent it from sticking to the kiln shelf, it is no disadvantage to leave the foot area unglazed.

It is difficult to immerse a really large and shallow bowl in the glaze bucket, and the best method is to pour glaze on to the outside from a jug. If the bowl has a good footring to hold on to, one hand can hold it while the other one pours. If not, the bowl will need supporting from the inside, which means pressure against the freshly glazed surfaces. Glaze normally dries quite swiftly on a biscuit pot, usually within a minute, and the dry powder which is left, though fragile, can be touched without harm. The bowl should either be supported by the fingertips, or placed on two steady rods over the glaze bucket.

Never touch a glazed surface which has not dried. It is sure to make marks just as a dog will make footprints on wet cement, and they cannot easily be touched up. When a glaze has completely dried on the pot, however, it can be touched very lightly with dry fingers to remove any ridges, and also to smooth over the reticulated pattern of cracks which sometimes shows up when a glaze is applied rather thickly on to a warm surface. When doing this, take care not to chip away sections of glaze – it is very fragile, especially on the rim. Handle the pot as little as possible, and make sure that no part of it is in contact with any other pot, either on the workroom shelf or in the kiln itself. Since glaze is molten glass in the kiln, it will stick to anything it touches in there. Glazed pots, therefore, must be kept apart, and glazed surfaces kept off the kiln shelves. The best way of doing this is to clean glaze off the bottoms of all pots with a wet sponge. In earthenware firings, pots can be raised on 'stilts' – tripods with fine points – so they can be glazed all over, and likewise plates are held in racks so that there is the minimum of contact with the glazed surface, At stoneware temperatures such structures cannot be relied upon not to warp, and studio potters tend to keep undersurfaces clean of glaze.

Glazing the outside of a cylinder

63

Glazing: principal and technique

Really complicated shapes are best glazed all in one dipping process, and it is a great help if you can hold on to the pot by some point near its base which does not need to be glazed. Handles can cause problems, but they can also help the potter, for if he holds the pot and dips the handle only into the bucket, he can use the handle, when it is dry, for its proper purpose when dipping the rest of the pot into the glaze. Teapots and all spouted ware must be glazed very carefully to ensure that pouring passages are free from glaze, and small unglazed areas are best touched up by dropping spots of glaze from a paintbrush rather than by re-dipping, which only adds unevenly to the glaze coat. You should bear in mind that the optimum thickness for most glazes is a powdery coat of about 2mm.

Organising yourself

A golden rule when glazing is to make sure that the vessels containing your glaze are big enough to give you room to manoeuvre the pot, and that you have enough glaze fully to submerge the pot if necessary without touching the bottom of the bucket – this kind of bump will mark and spoil the surface. It is also important that the vessel containing the glaze is itself large enough to cope with the displacement of glaze without overflowing when the pot is dipped into it. Glazing is a very messy business, and you should not try to do anything else at the same time. You are bound to splash glaze over the working surface, and you should keep other freshly made work out of the way. Only use one glaze at a time, carefully washing out sieves and bowls before sieving the next one.

If a spoonful of gum arabic or proprietary 'liquid binder' is added to a bowl of glaze, it can be brushed on to the surface of a biscuit or a dry, unfired pot with a soft housepainter's brush about 3cm wide. This technique is increasingly used with stoneware glazes, where the inevitably uneven coating often creates acceptable or even attractive variations in colour and texture.

The top picture shows a fingertip smoothing pinhole blemishes in the coating of glaze. The centre picture shows how a handle can be dipped in the glaze bucket. Left: glaze the inside of a spout by pouring through it, but do not forget later to unblock the straining holes.

8 Glazing: the finer points

Bowl by Lucie Rie

Glaze is rather like wine. The ingredients are abundant and cheap, and the process is a simple one. Yet the end product varies from the detestable to the sublime, and for roughly the same reasons as with wine. The quality of a glaze – surface, colour, texture and feel – is dependent on the trace elements, those aspects of its chemical composition present in minute quantities, and these can vary of course from batch to batch and from time to time. Glazes in industrial use can, and must, be made uniform by precise chemical control. Yet under the chemist's sterile scrutiny the glaze loses some of its soul, just as the highest quality factory-produced wine fails to match Chateau Latour. Only a handful of large firms, such as Meissen or Wedgwood, have been able to produce memorable, beautiful glazes, and the greatest ceramic treasures on Earth are the individual work of small potteries. The studio potter is, therefore, at an advantage. With his plastic bucket containing clay, wood ash and water, he may – just may – produce a masterpiece. It all depends on the trace elements in the clay and the ash. Some single materials such as felspar are capable of making a glaze all on their own, since they have enough alumina and silica to make glass, and enough potassium or sodium to 'flux' or accelerate its melting. Glazes are usually prepared by mixing various materials.

Earthenware glazes

In low temperature glazes the fluxes are usually lead or boron, and suppliers will sell these in a non-toxic insoluble form as a 'frit'. 'Lead frit' is simply lead which has been pre-heated to change its chemistry, and make a powder which is safe to handle without fear of poisoning. Used on its own a frit will make a very liquid runny glaze, and needs stabilising with some clayey materials such as china clay or felspar.

Transparent earthenware glazes are very useful for putting on slipware, where the pattern is to show through clearly. They can be coloured, as can all glazes, by adding metal oxides as follows:

Copper oxide for the blue-green
$\qquad$ 2% of dry weight of glaze
(Copper carbonate is half as strong, i.e. 4%)

Cobalt oxide for bright blue
$\qquad$ 0.5% of dry weight of glaze
(Cobalt carbonate is about half as strong, i.e. 1%)

Iron oxide for amber 4% of dry weight of glaze

Iron oxide for brown 8% of dry weight of glaze

Manganese oxide for purple brown
$\qquad$ 4% of dry weight of glaze

Tin oxide for white 8–10% of dry weight of glaze

Beginners seeking other colours such as orange and yellow would do best to use the colouring pigments prepared by the ceramic suppliers, since cadmium and uranium oxides which make such colours naturally are expensive or hard to come by.

Glazing: the finer points

Bright 'underglaze' colours from ceramic suppliers can look well on white clay under transparent glazes if used boldly and applied with a large brush. They work equally well in combination with an opaque white glaze, where a red body clay is as suitable as white. Earthenware glazes are made opaque by adding 8 to 10 per cent of tin oxide or zirconium to the dry weight of the glaze. All opaque glazes can be given a colour by adding an oxide in similar quantities to those quoted for transparent glazes, but the colours can differ markedly from those achieved with transparent glazes and the glazes become spotty if the oxides are not properly ground. It is a question of personal taste, but the total oxide content of the glaze should be kept below 12 per cent of the dry weight if possible.

The following three recipes for earthenware glazes can be used as a basis for experiment:

Medium Shiny   1060°C

Lead bisilicate	75
China stone	25

Shiny   1060°C
  (highly recommended)

Lead bisilicate	56
Felspar	30
China clay	7
Whiting	5

Matt   1060°C

Lead bisilicate	61
China stone	9
White body clay	20
Whiting	5
Bentonite	5

As a precaution against crazing (page 73) all pots have to be fired to a temperature above 1100°C. Since earthenware glazes mature at lower temperatures than this, the *biscuit* firing for earthenware pots must be taken to a temperature of at least 1100°C.

Stoneware glazes

The high temperatures for biscuit firings are unnecessary for stoneware glazes, since the pot will pass through the vital 1100°C barrier on its way up to the vitrification temperature of the glaze. Thus pots destined for stoneware are often fired to temperatures below 1000°C for the biscuit firing, which is more economical and makes them more porous when glazing.

There are almost as many glaze recipes as there are potters, and many books deal exclusively with the subject. It can all become rather bewildering, especially as identical ingredients are often given several different names. The enthusiastic beginner, eager for experiment, will soon find that recipes often do not live up to their description. This is not necessarily because of some fault on the part of the 'cook', as with recipes in the kitchen, but because of chemical variations in the materials, and these are hard to check without analysis. On supplier's felspar may be sufficiently different from another's to change the result significantly, and from the same supplier one batch may differ from the next. This is why even the most experienced potters talk with regret about 'lost' glazes which never come right any more, even though the recipe is followed scrupulously.

Lead and boron fluxes are not suitable for stoneware, as they become too runny at high temperatures, and disappear into the kiln atmosphere. Instead, potassium and sodium are used to get the melting process going, and with a high proportion of flux the glaze will be shiny. The mineral felspar, which keeps on cropping up in recipes, contains both fluxes, and is often called 'potash felspar' or 'soda felspar' according to which element is dominant. It does not matter very much which you use.

By increasing the clay (alumina and silica) content of the glaze, the shininess can also be reduced, and china clay, whiting (calcium carbonate) and talc (magnesium silicate) all

Slip-cast porcelain bowl by Ruth Duckworth, glazed in porcelain ash glaze (see page 72).

Well-organised workshops have glaze and oxide tes[ts] clearly labelled. By painting the name i[n] the oxide itself ther[e] can be no doubt about its identity. T[he] flat tests left show the way glazes and colourants behave [on] a smooth tile-like surface.

The thrown glaze tests right show how the glazes look on a curved surface. In the middle is silky white (see page 71), and on the lower left a range of ash glazes. Bryan Newman's glaze No 1 (see page 102) is shown below, flanked by variations of his glaze No 4.

Shoji Hamada, the greatest potter of this century, died in 1978 at the age of 83. He made this masterly bowl with wax-resist decoration and sang-de-boeuf glaze when in his twenties.

Withdrawn from the raku kiln still glowing and fiery, and quenched in water, the pot above shows a full range of colour from the copper and tin additions to the alkaline glaze described on page 77. Below: a tea bowl by Koetsu Honami. Cracked and richly mended with gold lacquer, the glaze flows from its rim like melting snow.

help to make matt glazes. Dolomite (magnesium carbonate) gives mattish glazes with a characteristic texture, and many of the ingredients commonly used in stoneware glaze formulae contain a combination of different fluxes.

The following recipes provide interesting and reliable glazes for domestic pots, across a wide spectrum of colour and texture. These glazes and others are illustrated in colour on page 68. Bear in mind that stoneware glazes are less bright in colour than earthenware, and that reduction atmospheres in wood, gas and oil kilns will alter the colours, usually making them colder and more interesting. More glaze recipes are given in Chapters 9, 10, 11 and 12, having been contributed by the authors as especially suitable to the techniques being described.

Oatmeal   1250°C

Potash felspar	49
China clay	25
Dolomite	22
Whiting	4

A glaze with a waxy surface. It is widely known and used. Looks well with cobalt oxide painting, which turns mauve.

Dark brown   1250°C

Felspar	53
Whiting	14
China clay	14.5
Flint	10.5
Iron	8

A dark brown glaze with a velvety texture. It is excellent for tableware, provided it is applied quite thickly.

Abrey crackle   1250°C

Felspar	40
Whiting	30
Powdered body clay	25
Ball clay	25
Cobalt oxide	0.25
Green nickel oxide	0.5
Titanium dioxide	5

From the recipe book of an old metallurgist who delighted in its speckly surface – the effect of titanium.

Silky white   1250°C

Felspar	50
Zinc oxide	22
Whiting	10
Tin oxide	8

A strong white, superb on porcelain.

Ash glazes

The remains of wood fires are rich in potassium, provided the ash is collected before it has rained. The method of collecting and preparing it is described in Chapter 12, and for glazes on domestic ware it should be sieved through a 100 mesh lawn. It is a powerful flux.

The **classic ash glaze** formula is:

Wood ash	40
Felspar	40
Ball clay	20

Firing range 1240°–1260°C

The colour of this glaze, and also its surface qualities, will depend on the trace elements in the wood ash, as explained at the beginning of this chapter, but the colour spectrum is generally from greenish-grey to honey-yellow.

Second ash glaze formula   1250°C

Felspar	50
Wood ash	30
Flint	10
China clay	7
Iron oxide	10

This ash glaze will inevitably be brown because of the iron oxide, but according to the mineral content of the ash it is usually blotched with golden spots.

Glazing: the finer points

Charterhouse tenmoku   1250°C

Quartz	40.8
Felspar	22.5
Iron oxide	12
Whiting	11.2
Wood ash	8
China clay	5.6

This dark brown glaze is described in Chapter 16, and illustrated on page 126. It is better if 'reduced'.

Porcelain ash glaze   1280°C

Felspar	40
China clay	38
Whiting	20
Wood ash	15–20
Copper oxide	0.1
(for turquoise, see page 103, lower picture)	
Iron oxide	1.0
(for duck egg blue)	

A glaze which often turns white on sharp edges, like bone showing through skin (see page 67).

There is a big difference between a glaze which is matt because of its ingredients and one which is matt because it has been underfired. The latter – hard to the touch and grainy – is unmistakable and invariably unpleasant. A matter of 10°C is all that is necessary to transform a hard unrewarding surface into a poem, and it is essential to observe the exact firing temperatures indicated for a recipe. Pyrometers (high temperature thermometers) are not usually accurate to 10°C, but seger cones or their equivalents placed to be viewed through the spyhole of the kiln will indicate by bending over exactly how much heat-work has been done, and thus tell the vigilant potter when to turn off. If you can retain this temperature by turning the kiln down a little, you will 'soak' the pots, which often means an improvement in the glaze. If you exceed the temperature the glaze will probably go runny, or start to bubble.

Over-firing is only one of the many problems which are encountered in glazing, but it usually means the pots sticking to the kiln shelves.

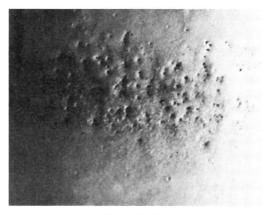

Pinholing is sometimes prized.

Pinholing of the surface is caused by gases bubbling out of the glaze or even the body, and it can sometimes be overcome by soaking the glaze for half an hour or so (see above), though this may change the quality of the glaze in other ways.

Crawling of the glaze is a common and maddening fault. The cause of this is either dust or grease on the biscuit surface, or fine cracking of the glaze surface prior to firing. It is overcome by keeping biscuit pots scrupulously clean and smoothing over the glaze with a dry fingertip, if cracks appear, thereby pushing glaze particles in between the cracks like grout in between tiles.

When a biscuit pot is dusty or too dry the glaze coat will not adhere, and in extreme cases will fall off before it even reaches the kiln.

Bloating is always ugly.

Bloating is not really a glaze fault, but usually happens in the glaze firing. The cause of this ugly blistering is gas forming within the body clay, and this most frequently happens when clays have been carelessly mixed, or contain impurities.

Crazing is the commonest fault of all, and consists of minute cracks occurring all over the glaze surface, because the clay body has contracted less than the glaze on cooling. It is very difficult to find a stoneware glaze which exactly fits the body clay, and the more glassy the glaze, the more likely, or at least the more conspicuous, the crazing. Crazing can happen quickly if pots are taken too hot from a kiln, but it

Poor adhesion or cracking before firing will cause crawling, when the glaze shrinks back into thick beads, leaving part of the biscuit surface bare.

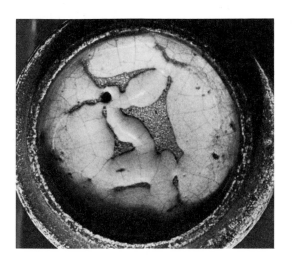

Blistering from the overlapping of incompatible glazes is impractical for tableware. The blisters often burst and the edges are sharp.

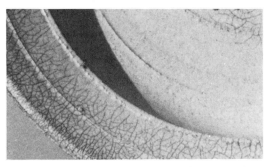

Crazing always happens in a raku kiln, and can be emphasised by rubbing in oxides.

often happens slowly, over several months. The addition of flint, or any other material that is known to contract little on cooling, can help the glaze, but it will also change it, so additions must be made cautiously.

Glazes behave differently, of course, on different clays: imagine the permutations that would give you a complete range of glazes on a complete set of clays; far too many to keep in your head. It is as well, though, to test glazes on more than one clay. I try to make two glaze tests of each batch of glaze I prepare, one on a coarse buff stoneware and one on a white porcellanic clay. A group of tests, shaped like little bottles, and with bases wide enough for recorded information below, is shown on page 68. If you do something similar, make sure that at the same time as naming the glaze test, you also identify the glaze bucket with the same name or number in indelible ink.

73

Section Two – Abstract and Decorative Pottery

9 Raku
by Gerry Harvey

Winter-moon tea bowl by Koho Kangetsu

In the wide spectrum of ceramics, raku occupies a small but rather spectacular place. Like Ikebana in the village flower-arranging show, a mental jerk is necessary: preconceived ideas and dogma are discarded. Raku is the experience of glazing ceramic articles of some durability very quickly in an improvised kiln at low temperatures. Irregularity of form and unevenness of glaze are unavoidable; the fire makes its mark. The result is not necessarily crude, but it may be so, and worthless. On the other hand, it can be fine. The rakuist's art is closer to that of the glass blower . . . Gerry Harvey explains the process.

Raku, which has its origins in Japan, means joyfulness. The process was used in the making of bowls and dishes for the tea ceremony. The immediacy and robustness of the method, the excitement and surprises inherent in this process do indeed make it a joyful adventure. The whole story of making a pot, the shaping from earth and water, the transformation by fire unfolds before the eyes in minutes. To draw a pot from the red-hot kiln, cover it in sawdust, then lift it still smouldering to quench it in water to create its colour and texture is always a moment of sheer magic to the potter.

Clay

It is possible to dig clay from your garden and by preparation make it suitable for raku pots, and many fascinating experiments can be made in this way. For most people beginning raku, it is simpler to use ready-prepared clay. Suppliers produce special clays for raku, but any standard stoneware clay can be adapted fairly simply. What you need is a clay which is robust and 'open' enough to withstand the thermal shock of being put into a red-hot kiln and then, after firing, of being cooled rapidly by immersion in water. To achieve this you must have a clay with a total grog content of between 30 per cent and 40 per cent. A grog which contains coarse to medium particles (30–60 mesh) is best and if this is first moistened with water it can be kneaded into the clay by spreading a handful at a time on to a table and rolling the clay into it. Soon there is no need to weigh out the grog: one gets to understand by the look and feel of the clay how much is needed. The clay must be kneaded until the grog is evenly spread, and this can be checked by cutting through the clay lump with a wire. As a guide, 50g of grog weighed dry and added to 500g of plastic clay will give a suitable mixture.

Shaping

The character of the special clay that is used for raku, and the thermal shock given to it in the kiln, considerably affect the range of shapes possible. The traditional raku tea bowls, modest in form and perhaps crude to Western eyes, reveal in their simplicity a beauty that directly springs from the technique. Traditionally these bowls are shaped by pinching between the thumb and fingers (see Chapter 10 Pinch-built Pottery) and were in two distinct styles: for the practical reason that Japanese tea houses are

Raku

Winter mode

Summer mode

becomes painful to the hands. Raku bodies are not as plastic as normal clays and throwing must be very swift and direct to prevent collapse or tearing of the wall. Remember that robust and simple forms tend to be the most successful.

Irregular raku pots can be made from thrown forms, after they have stiffened slightly, by 'paddling' them with the hands or a flat piece of wood (see below). Most squared off raku pots are produced like this and if the tool used has a pattern, a surface texture is given to the pot.

Remember that the pots have to be placed into a small red-hot kiln with tongs and so they cannot

Paddled form

unheated in winter, those of the 'winter style', are closed in to keep the tea warm and to fit the hands comfortably. In summer this is not necessary and the shape is wide and shallower. The colours, too, follow the seasons, being sombre in winter and bright in summer.

Most of the usual techniques employed in building pots can be used successfully for raku. Pinching can be extended by joining two forms together, or coils can be added to a pinched base. 'Plunge pots', where a batten of wood is pressed directly into a block of clay and the sides sliced away with a wire, are very suitable as their internal structure is amorphous and they withstand well the stresses of raku firing. Slab-building, although possible, needs extra care because of the method of forming, and joins must be efficiently made and the pot dried very slowly to lessen the stresses of warping.

Raku pots can also be made on the wheel though the clay must not be too coarse, A finer grog should be mixed in, otherwise throwing

Plunge pot by Bryan Newman

be too large. This means that an even minimum thickness of 6mm is required, with substantial rims to withstand the pressure of the tongs. Closed-in and bottle-shaped forms also cause problems and tend to shatter on plunging into water, unless this is done very slowly, with the opening upwards. What will survive is an obvious criterion, and undoubtedly experience is a hard teacher.

Bisc

Raku pots are biscuited in the normal way. Electric kilns are probably the most convenient, but if no other kiln is available, the biscuit firing can be done, as it was traditionally, in the raku kiln itself (see page 79). Because of its small size, this has a disadvantage in that only a few pots can be fired at a time.

The usual precautions for biscuit firing must be observed: a slow gradual climb in temperature until 500°C is reached. The temperature for this first firing should be between 900° and 950°C. A correctly fired pot must have sufficient strength to withstand handling by the raku tongs but must be open and porous enough to enable it to absorb the raku glaze thickly.

Glazes

Glazes for raku should be so designed to melt between 750° and 1000°C. Traditionally, raku glazes were very low temperature, but today potters tend to fire to the higher end of this range, so that a stronger and more durable pot is possible. The glazes themselves are usually simple and it is better to get to know one or two well than to experiment with recipe after recipe. The rich colour and texture so characteristic of raku pottery comes not so much from a complexity of glazes, but from the treatment given to the pot after it is taken from the kiln.

The original raku glazes were based principally on raw lead, which is very poisonous both before and after firing, so modern raku glazes are usually based upon frits which enable lead to be used more safely. Most ceramic suppliers have these frits in their catalogues.

Recipes

All these ingredients are obtainable from the suppliers listed on page 133.

Alkaline glazes

Clear glazes

High alkaline frit	93
China clay	4
Bentonite	3

To create colour, add

3% copper oxide	turquoise
0.25–0.5% cobalt	blue
1–2% manganese	purple
5% tin oxide	white (double dip)

High alkaline frits are safe to use and develop exciting glaze colours that can be obtained in no other way. They are some of the brightest and most pure colours in pottery. Bentonite is used to help overcome the tendency for the glaze to settle quickly in the tub and to make the glaze coating less friable, or fragile.

Lead-based glazes

Clear glaze 1

Lead bisilicate	90
Flint	4
China clay	6

Clear glaze 2

| Lead sesquisilicate | 85 |
| Ball clay | 15 |

To create colour in either of these glazes, add
3% copper oxide	green
4–8% red iron	yellow/amber
5% tin	white
8% red iron / 3% manganese / 2% cobalt	black
8% red iron / 3% manganese	brown

When lead frits are used for raku, care should be taken not to inhale dust during preparation of the glaze.

The raku technique is rarely used these days for

functional pots, but just a word of caution about lead-based raku glazes. Because they are low fired, soft, and invariably crazed and therefore prone to attack from acids found in food and drink, they are unsuitable for functional wares. Copper oxide, which provides attractive colours in both alkaline and lead-based raku glazes, because of its toxicity should also be avoided for functional ware glazed in low temperature firing.

Most of the rules of glazing are broken when decorating raku pots. A big floppy brush applies a thick coat of a second glaze to encourage variety of colour and texture.

Raku glazes should be used thickly and can be dipped, poured, dribbled, splashed or brushed. The spontaneity of these methods is very much in the spirit of raku. Because glazes are used so thickly, often one on top of another, the glaze itself is brittle and it is easy to knock it off the pot before firing. Adding some Polycel paste to the mixture will help overcome this problem.

After glazing, the pots must be thoroughly dried or they will burst on being put into the kiln simply because the water absorbed during glazing expands as steam. The drying is usually done by placing them on top of the kiln as it is being warmed up.

The colours of raku glazes are drastically affected by the treatment given to the pot once it is removed from the kiln. Copper, for instance, will give a lovely turquoise in an alkaline base or

bright green in a lead base provided it is cooled, after removal from the kiln, in air where plenty of oxygen is available. The pot can be cooled slowly or quenched in water. On the other hand if, after removal from the kiln, oxygen is prevented from reaching the glaze by covering the pot with straw, leaves or sawdust, local 'reduction' takes place and metallic oxides such as copper will be starved of oxygen and reduced to their base metals. This will produce a metallic sheen or 'lustre' in the glaze. Other oxides like cobalt, iron or tin will also change surprisingly, though results are never quite as predictable. Tin gives a lovely pearly sheen in alkaline glazes.

Firing

Firing a raku kiln is, to say the least, hot and thirsty work, and as surfaces are very hot some special equipment and precautions are necessary for comfort and safety. Long-handled tongs and asbestos gloves, which can be bought from any of the ceramic suppliers, will protect from the extremes of heat and enable pots to be placed in and removed from the kiln safely. A small lidded metal dustbin will be needed, filled with combustible materials (straw, leaves, sawdust), to treat the pots after firing, as well as a metal bucket in which to cool the pots by quenching.

Firing single-handed presents difficulties, and a second person to remove the kiln shelf or bat which acts as a door whilst the pots are being placed or removed is fairly essential, especially if great heat loss from the kiln is to be avoided. This assistant will also need gloves and tongs for protection.

The rakuist places his first pots carefully in the kiln, his assistant closing the door as quickly as possible to retain the heat. The time taken for firing varies from 20 to 25 minutes for the first kiln load to perhaps 10 minutes for later loads as the kiln builds up heat. The potter watches carefully through the spy-hole in the opposite side of the chamber until the pots are shiny and glowing with an even glazed surface. Remember they look shinier and more fluxed in the kiln than they actually are.

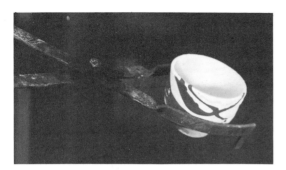

Pincers adapted to hold pots before firing

The pots are then ready, and using the tongs the potter withdraws them one by one from the glowing kiln, holding each for a few seconds to allow the glaze to settle and then plunging it into the sawdust. The assistant can put the lid on the bin, remembering that it gets hot, otherwise the sawdust will flame rather than smoulder. The longer the pot is in the sawdust the heavier the reduction. Normally the time of reduction is between two and five minutes. Reduction causes violent smoking and therefore must be done in the open air.

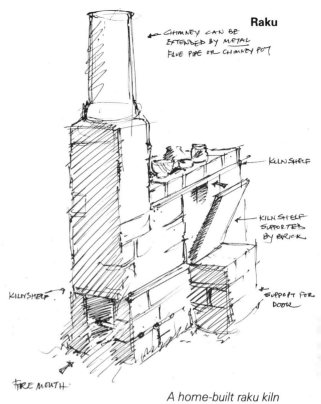

A home-built raku kiln

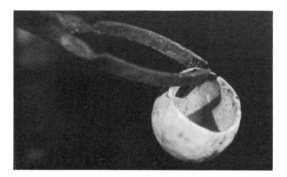

Pincers hold a red-hot pot on its way to the sawdust bucket, as shown right.

To freeze-in the reduction, the potter immediately quenches his pot in water as soon as it is removed from the sawdust. The pot will have collected sawdust on its surface from the reduction, so when it is cool it must be scrubbed to reveal its full texture and colour. Partial reduction can be achieved by covering only part of the pot with sawdust, and here, depending on how efficiently the glaze is starved of oxygen, the colour produced will vary from metallic sheen to lighter effects where the reduction is less complete.

Raku

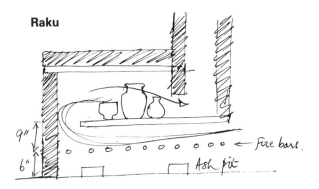

The wood-fired raku kiln measures approximately a metre from front to back. The chimney must be at least a metre high.

Most pots that come from the kiln are homely pieces with the occasional crack or distortion, but there is always that exciting moment when 'treasure' is revealed: a beautiful pot with a completely satisfying shape and subtle colour and textures.

The kiln

The kiln can be built in the garden with ordinary bricks, using a thin mortar of 50 per cent fireclay plus 50 per cent grog or sand. It will be temporary as the bricks will eventually suffer from the effects of heat. For a more permanent structure firebricks should be used.

Undoubtedly, wood is the most spectacular fuel to use, and at the height of the fire its long flame will lick right through the kiln and shoot out of the top of the chimney. It is very important that the wood used should not be too large. Pieces of dry wood about 30–60cm long and 3–5cm in diameter are ideal. The idea is to stoke 'little and often' to ensure a steady climb in temperature, and it is of necessity a full-time job. Fired in this way, a small kiln should reach glazing temperature in about two to three hours.

Using a powerful flame gun of the kind sold to clear paths of weeds, such as the Sheen 600, the temperature can be reached somewhat quicker, though it will be necessary speedily to refuel the gun at times. Having wood handy at this time will enable the kiln temperature to be kept up during refuelling.

Raku bowl 18cm in diameter by Jane Waller

10 Pinch-built pottery

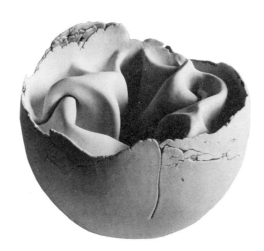

by Mary Rogers

There is no doubt that it is in the field of hand-modelled ceramics – vessels and sculptural pieces small in scale and made entirely without machinery – that there have been the biggest developments and changes in recent years. From being the Cinderella of pottery, often left behind at primary school, pinched and hand-made forms, often in porcelain, are now amongst the most spectacular of ceramics made all over the world. One of the artists principally responsible, through the beauty of her own work, for this revolution of attitudes, is Mary Rogers, who here contributes a chapter on the pinch-building technique.

Pinch-building is a very simple and basic way of making pottery. It is probably the earliest used by man, being an almost instinctive method of forming a hollow shape from a lump of clay. It can be done without any tools at all, just the hands, and with clay of any sort. Even a highly finished piece made by this method needs only very simple tools, and then not to form it, but only to give the final surface a smooth finish. It is also a very quiet and satisfying method of working, demanding gentleness of touch combined with concentration. The work proceeds slowly and rhythmically and seems to grow with a natural inevitability.

Starting a pinched pot

A lump of clay, large enough for the finished piece, and thoroughly wedged to remove any air bubbles, is patted roughly into a sphere. This is then held in one hand and rotated whilst the thumb of the other hand is gently pushed into its centre, using the pad of the thumb rather than the tip. Then, whilst the ball of clay is still being slowly turned, the bottom of the initial hollow is rounded with the curve of the thumb, and so the base of the pot is made.

Forming the base

To a large extent the final form which the pot can take is determined at this point. The walls of the pot will grow from the base and so it must be made the right shape for the kind of pot envisaged. If, for example, the base is to be broad, shallow and widely curving, then the pot is held in the palm of one hand while the base is gradually pinched and smoothed outwards with the thumb of the other hand. But if the base is to be small and deep, then the pot is rested over a finger of one hand, and the clay is thinned by pressing from the outside with the thumb of the other hand. The base should be pinched out to its final thinness at this initial stage and then the forming of the walls may begin.

Forming of walls

The walls are gradually thinned and raised with a circling movement, gently pressing the clay between the finger and thumb, each higher circle of pinched depressions slightly overlapping the previous ones. The main aim is to keep the pressure between the fingers and thumb even, and the spaces between each squeeze equal. The pace of the work is one of slow relaxed concentration, there is no need to hurry. In fact the drying out which happens as the clay is thinned slowly in the warmth of the

Pinch-built pottery

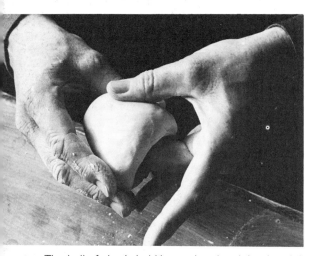

The ball of clay is held in one hand and the thumb is pressed in the centre. The bottom is rounded out and the walls are formed by gentle pressure between finger and thumbs.

hands can be helpful, in that it gives stability to the clay by making it less plastic as it becomes thinner, taller and wider.

For a small shape, or a thick one, one journey from the base and around the walls to the rim may be sufficient, but if a larger piece is being made, or egg-shell thinness is being aimed at, then the circles of indentations may be worked over again, concentrating this time on pressing out the slightly raised ridges between the rows. As the clay walls become larger and floppier it may help to hold the growing shape on its side whilst working, and to support the soft walls on the wrist of the supporting hand. Or the piece may be rested upside down on its rim to stiffen up a little and returned to later. Often it is best to work on two or three pots at a time so that work is not interrupted while pots are left to stiffen up. If a fairly thick wall is being thinned out the excess clay can be smoothed up the walls from the base to the top of both the outside and the inside. If the profile of the pot is to be an inward-turning curve then the top must be squeezed inwards gently, or 'collared', between each round of pinching to make it smaller. This usually causes slight creases in the clay near the rim and these should be smoothed out before pinching is resumed.

Circles of finger indentations proceed up and around the walls to the rim.

Excess clay is eased up the walls.

Forming the rim

As the pot form grows the variations in height of the rim edge will begin to emerge. These can be left as evidence of how the pot grew from an uneven ball of clay, or they can be cut off to give a more even edge. This can be done with a needle, a blade, or even scissors.

When the clay is being eased gently outwards it often splits at the edge. This can be prevented, if wished, by constantly rounding off the rim throughout the work. But it can be very attractive, and so encouraged, and even emphasised by extra pinching which will make the delicately splitting edge a decorative feature.

Drying out the pot

When the main form is finished it may still be too soft to hold its own shape without support, and so it must be rested in something which will not deform it. This may be done in many improvised ways. For example, it can be rested in a cup or some other container with an outward-curving rim which will not cut into the soft walls of the piece. Or it can be hung over a round object, such as a ball, which should be covered with a piece of nylon to prevent the clay from sticking to it. Or it can be placed in a bowl larger than itself, with pieces of foam holding the soft clay in place as it dries. This last method is particularly useful when a very irregular form is being made. If, however, the walls are fairly stiff by the time

the form is finished, then the only problem is to prevent the pot's own weight from depressing the upward curve from the base. This can be done by standing it on a piece of dry sponge, rather than a hard surface, for further drying out and stiffening.

Adding a footring

If a footring is needed to complete the pot, it is best added when the clay is leather-hard. The ring is made by rolling or pinching out a piece of clay into a strip. This is mitred at each end, and is then joined into a ring with slurry, a paste made from some of the clay with which one is working, mixed with water. (Powdered clay is better than plastic clay for making slurry.)

The slight asymmetry of the hand-built pot may mean that the point of balance is not necessarily in the centre of the base, and slight adjustments will have to be made to determine exactly where to place the footring. The position is then marked with a pencil or some other sharp object, and the slurry is dabbed on the top edge of the footring, which is then gently pressed on to the marked place on the base of the pot.

The hardening pot is carefully balanced on a prepared footring, taking into account its centre of gravity.

Pinch-built pottery

A wooden tool smooths the join.

A clean joint is made by means of a wooden modelling tool, and finally small rolls of soft clay are used to seal the joint on both the inside and the outside of the ring. The excess clay may be smeared into the base and the footring, giving a stronger joint and a smoother transition. The pot is then left to become leather-hard in the case of stoneware and earthenware, and completely dry in the case of porcelain, so that it is ready for scraping.

Tidying, smoothing and refining the form

This final finishing off of the surface is, of course, a matter of choice. When finger marks occur in a seemingly arbitrary manner and are intrusive in that they destroy the full sweep of the form, and look like dents, I find that they are best scraped down. But, of course it is not simply a matter of making the surface smooth. The scraping may also be treated as an opportunity to refine and perfect the form of the pot. The ideal tool for this is a metal kidney, and a face mask should be worn during the scraping so as to avoid breathing in the fine powder. The work is exacting, especially with porcelain, owing to the pot's fragility in the unfired state, and the piece must be held very delicately throughout.

Some suggestions for further development

It is possible with pinching, as with coiling, to elaborate the form and to build in the decoration in a great variety of ways as the work progresses. The possibility for experimentation is endless. For example, as the pinching progresses, or when the main form is leather-hard, strips and pieces of extra clay can be joined to the main body with slip, in the same way that lugs and handles are added to casseroles and mugs, and these can then be pinched out into fins and frills, wings and double rims.

Pinched out shapes can be combined. For example, two pinched bowls may be joined together to give a closed sphere with a hollow interior. To do this two equal-sized hemispheres are stood on their edges to stiffen just a little, then the edges are scored and slurry is dabbed on to them. They are then pressed together rim to rim and slightly screwed into place to make a good join. The excess clay and slurry is then smeared over each opposite hemisphere. It is usually a good idea to add an extra collar of soft clay around the join and to blend this into each side to give a really good firm joint. Whilst there

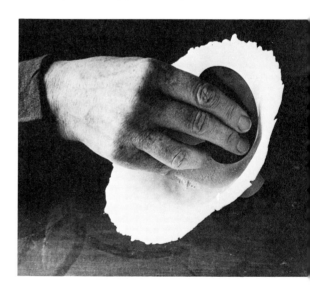

A metal kidney is used to smooth and refine the form.

*Convoluted bowl with perforations,
by Mary Rogers*

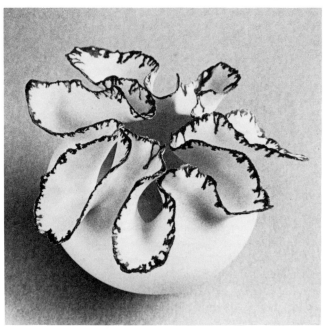

*A pinched convoluted mouth to a thrown porcelain
sphere by Deirdre Burnett*

Pinch-built pottery

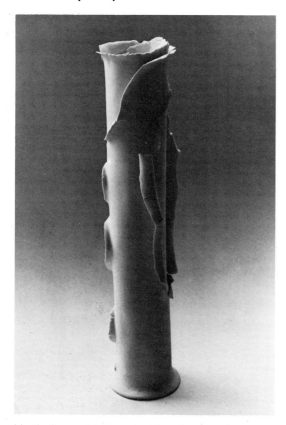

Vertical porcelain form by Mary Rogers

with the pinching process one's imagination expands, and experimentation becomes almost second nature, so that a very personal form of self-expression can develop through this use of clay.

Glazes

It is important to choose glazes which are complementary to the fine detail and small scale of pinched pottery. The following recipes are recommended.

Stoneware   (matt white) 1250°–1260°C

Felspar	48
Dolomite	19
China clay	27
Quartz	3
Bone ash	3

Porcelain   1250°–1300°C

Felspar	40
Flint	28
Whiting	22
China clay	10

Pinch bowl with inlaid decoration and small base

is air trapped inside the ball it may be rolled around, flattened and faceted and textured in many different ways. The trapped air gives it the strength to withstand this rough treatment without collapsing. Finally, of course, the air will have to be let out through a small hole which can be made with a needle. The hole must be left so that the air can escape during firing, otherwise the sphere will burst.

Different coloured clays may be wedged together and then pinched into shape to give built-in colour and pattern. Discs, spots and stripes of coloured clays may be inlaid into the main form, a groove having been cut out and the different clay or slip laid into this. Or the walls may be textured, pierced and carved. If the piece is to be carved, thick areas can be left during the pinching to allow extra depth for the carving.

These and many other ways of working will come to mind. In fact as one becomes confident

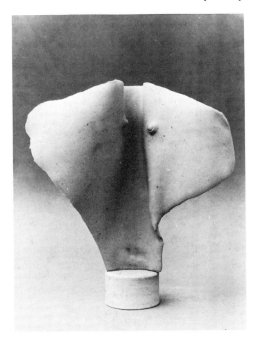

Pinched porcelain form by Ruth Duckworth

Below: hollow pod form with pierced top made by joining two pinched bowls together, and carving the decoration. Porcelain, by Mary Rogers.

Cloud-edged bowl by Mary Rogers, with controlled crawling decoration

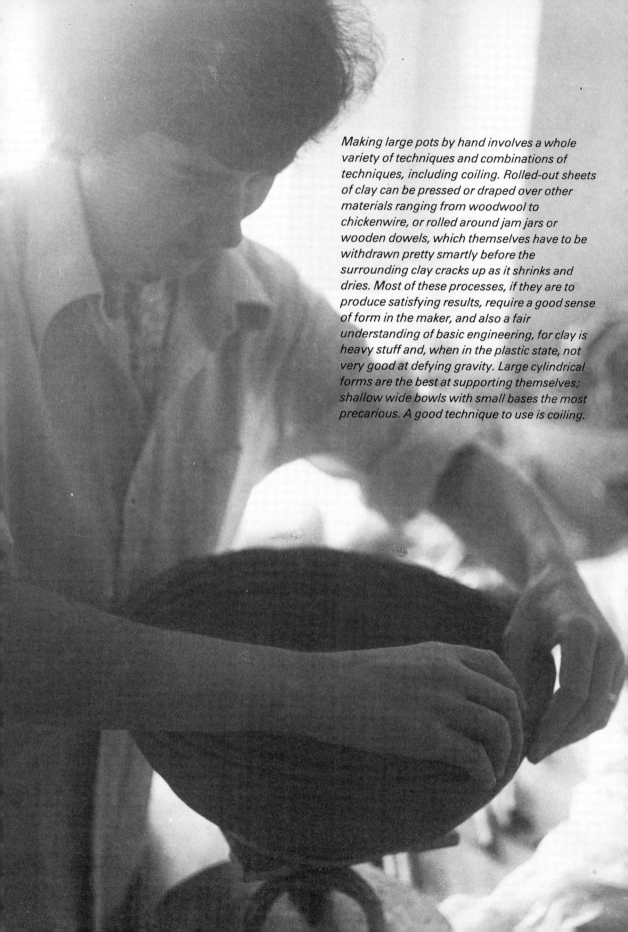

Making large pots by hand involves a whole variety of techniques and combinations of techniques, including coiling. Rolled-out sheets of clay can be pressed or draped over other materials ranging from woodwool to chickenwire, or rolled around jam jars or wooden dowels, which themselves have to be withdrawn pretty smartly before the surrounding clay cracks up as it shrinks and dries. Most of these processes, if they are to produce satisfying results, require a good sense of form in the maker, and also a fair understanding of basic engineering, for clay is heavy stuff and, when in the plastic state, not very good at defying gravity. Large cylindrical forms are the best at supporting themselves; shallow wide bowls with small bases the most precarious. A good technique to use is coiling.

11 Coiling

Most beginners know that a 'coil' or 'rope' of clay is an ancient and very functional building unit for large pots and from prehistoric times has been used effectively with great beauty in creating massive storage vessels for wine and grain. Such big, bellying forms (see picture on page 6) need to be strong to withstand the huge pressures from inside when filled up. They were often decorated simply with wavy rope-like shapes or ribbons which derived directly from the technique by which the pots are made.

Some cultures in Africa still make the majority of their domestic pots by coiling, and in the madding complexity of modern ceramics in the West, the beginner may well discover in coil pottery a touchstone where he can find simplicity and strength of form. Coiled pots are slow to make and difficult to make well. They lack the symmetrical discipline of the wheel-made pots, but are probably the most sensual of all ceramics, with a strong tactile appeal.

The technique of rolling out the coils and joining them one above the other in rings is explained below the accompanying illustrations, and is not difficult. The beginner can very easily come unstuck, however, if he tries to make the wrong sort of shape. It is attractive and sensible to make large coiled pots, as large as the kiln can take. To make a small, fiddly thing with little worm-like coils is to waste the opportunity of hefty vigour that the technique offers. A thrown pot as tall as a tuba would be beyond any beginner in pottery, but size is on the potter's side in coiling.

It is tempting to make shapes which cannot be made on the wheel – with triangular or cigar-shaped bases. Resist it; it is better to think of fruit-like shapes, forms which fatten up from inside like gourds or apples. Concave surfaces as well as convex ones can be effectively made with coils, but natural changes from one curve to another are usually better than hard-edged ones.

Unfortunately, although coiled pots give excellent opportunity for surface decoration, large forms can often be boring, especially if they are tentative. A mushroom-like shape, for instance, interesting if it is no bigger than your fist, can look like something which has strayed out of Snow White if it is made very large, and large surfaces adorned with fins or applied excrescences to relieve surface boredom often look ridiculous. If there is to be ornamentation of the surface with relief, this must be planned when the pot is conceived in your mind, rather than as it nears completion.

It is *always* a good idea to have a clear image of the finished shape, and this will help you through the tedious early stage, when most coil pots look much the same. Changing the shape of the pot by increasing or decreasing the size of the coil rings, to make the pot larger or smaller, must be done with circumspection, for the coiled pot will readily sag, especially outwards, and this is why bellying forms are so often made inside plaster moulds for support, with footrings added later, as shown on page 83. Any sympathetic method of support can be used to

Coiling

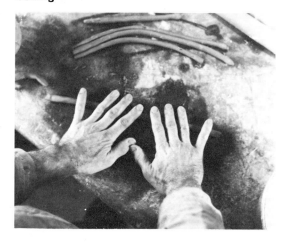

shore up a coiled form that wants to sit down –
buttresses of clay, sponges, 'nests' of cloth, but
one of the best ways is the natural method of
making the pot slowly so that the clay in the
lower regions hardens up enough to support the
floppier part higher up.

Enclosed, near-spherical shapes, like massive
pebbles, are very strong and often effective if
the surface is sensibly handled (they must have
a small hole somewhere, or they will burst in the
kiln).

If the top of the pot is rounded like a church
dome, it will support itself well, even if there is a
small hole at the centre. Trouble starts,
however, if you try to build a tall neck on top of
such a shape, as the weight may press the top
down into an ugly and unintentional
depression. Filling the pot up with newspaper,

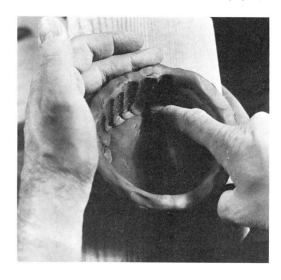

*Roll out sausages of wedged clay on a dry surface.
The length of the coil you will make is determined by
the span of your hands when spread widely apart
with the thumbs touching. Roll the clay backwards
and forwards under your hands until it is round in
section. If a coil starts to take on a flattened section,
stop and pat it with your fingers into a more
symmetrical shape, and carry on rolling. Add coils in
regular rings, rather than in a continuous spiral. Butt
the ends together carefully and press the coils down.
When you have laid three or four on top of one
another, reinforce the joins by rubbing downwards
with a fingertip or a tool inside and outside to bond
the coils together.*

crumpled up so that it is still springy, is a good way of giving support from the inside, and this will of course burn away in the kiln.

I personally dislike the tell-tale bulges of the coils showing on the finished form, and prefer to smooth or texture the visible surfaces using fingers or a wooden or metal tool. A piece of unplaned wood used as a beater will create a craggy surface appropriate to large pots. Clay fragments or strips can be beaten on, to give a double surface to the work either in a random way or in a repeating pattern. Hardboard 'combs', hacksaw blades or textured tools such as old-fashioned butter-pat-makers can be helpful. The potter's 'handwriting' is all over a coiled pot's surface, especially if he uses only his fingers to achieve the final texture. Finger marks on the surface can be very attractive, but are not always so. Remember that any texturing

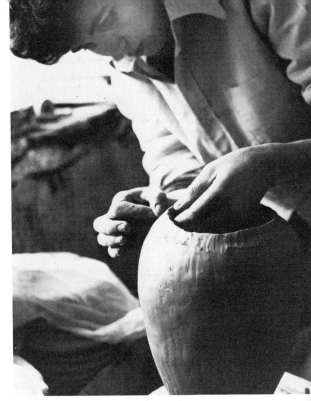

When the surface is textured with a fingertip or modelling tool, the lines of coils disappear. The texture is up to you, and it is worth trying a variety of tools, including a comb.

It is often necessary to support the wall with one hand while texturing the clay with the other one, as shown above, especially when making open forms which are inclined to sag under their own weight.

Round forms make good coiled pots.

on the surface can be emphasised by applying a colourant with a sponge to deepen the shadows and the crevices.

A good thick, rounded rim at the top of the pot will usually be an asset. Some coiled pots, like the magnificent Pueblo pots from New Mexico (see pages 4 and 125) can get away with thin rims, but full, rounded forms need a decisive punctuation mark and help the pot to come to an end. The point at which to end a coiled pot is one of the decisions beginners often find difficult. This decision is taken in advance with wheel-made or slab-built pots, for it depends on the amount of clay being used. If this particular problem does raise its head, it is best answered by carrying on with the form until you have gone *too* far, until the pot looks attenuated. Then remove a few coils till the form looks comfortable again.

Coiling: design

Some people are natural coilers, and for such people advice about form is unnecessary. They will progress from one shape to another and will

probably make 'families' of coiled pots, all different yet all the same, like pebbles on the beach or marrows on the show-bench. Beginners will sometimes make a coiled pot simply in order to have the technique under their belt, and perhaps they have no clear idea of what kind of pot it should be. Functional ware is best made by other methods, partly because the nature of coiling implies large size and heaviness. For those unwilling or not confident enough to follow their fingers in whatever sculptural direction they are taken, I recommend large fruit bowls and large flower vases as subjects.

Glazes

Shiny glazes tend to emphasise minor irregularities of surfaces, and can have a disruptive effect on the coil pot. Matt or semi-matt glazes, especially in stoneware, tend to vary in colour as they vary in thickness and this is not necessarily a disadvantage on the coiled pot. Raw glazing can work well with the coiling technique. This is the application of a glaze coat to an unfired pot and the result is often harmonious, although the technique sometimes causes problems in the kiln. You must be absolutely sure that your raw-glazed pot is bone-dry before it goes into the kiln, and the kiln must be heated up slowly, as for a biscuit firing. A raw-glazed coiled pot which explodes and sticks itself to other students' work in a mixed firing is very unpopular and anti-social.

Glazes containing dolomite and rutile have a slightly granular surface which I think is well suited to coiled pottery, and there is, of course, a strong tradition of finishing coiled pots with a burnished surface of graphite or a strong colourant. Any painted decoration on the coiled pots needs to be strong and bold, especially as the surface is often bumpy, but painting is generally less sympathetic to the technique than are textural patterns – see Chapter 16.

Suggested glaze formulae

A coiled pot rolled in wood ash while still damp will produce a glazed coating which may have an interesting texture and colour, although such a pot is unlikely to be water-tight; it needs a reliable glaze for the inside if you want to be able to fill it up with liquid.

Ash glazes

The basic formula given on page 71 is suitable for all coiled pots. It can be modified with countless variations.

Dark green ash glaze   1250°C

Wood ash	30
Cornish stone	30
Ball clay	15
Copper oxide	2
Cobalt oxide	2
Iron oxide	2
Titanium oxide	7

An evil, dark green, because of the heavy loading of oxide, and often with an interesting texture, thanks to the titanium. It makes a very nice contrast to the normal sandy colour of stoneware clay in oxidised firing and is thus useful for pots which are only partially glazed. It must be used thickly for the best effect.

Talc glaze   1250°C

Talc	30
Felspar	34
Whiting	25
Flint	11
Rutile	2

A useful glaze with a good grain, inclined to bubble *attractively* when thick. Rather like varnish when thin. Works well with iron.

Pinkish white   1250°C

Felspar	61
China clay	6
Whiting	14
Barium carbonate	11
Magnesium carbonate	2.5
Rutile	5.5

Partially opaque glaze, often speckled, which I find handsome on the inside surface of large coiled forms.

If you do not have access to stoneware or high-firing, try the earthenware glazes described on page 66, or leave the outside of the pot with a burnished or oxide-coated finish. Glazes which are known to craze can be used to handsome effect on thrown pottery, but crazing does not particularly suit the coiled technique and you should avoid these glazes wherever possible.

Massive coiled pot by Ruth Duckworth, coated in manganese oxide to give a metallic purple.

12 Slab-building

by Bryan Newman

Bryan Newman, one of the best-known modern exponents of creative slab pottery, describes here his personal methods and ideas.

I am very wary about saying, 'this is *the* way to make slab pots.' There are always so many ways. I know my way works for me, giving me the results I am looking for, but I have met many potters who use totally different methods successfully.

There are many techniques for making clay slabs. You can roll them out like pastry or you can cut them from a block of clay like sawing boards from a tree trunk. They can be joined together very wet or quite dry. Often the technique used alters the feeling of the piece; sometimes it just suits your personality.

◀ *Slab sculpture by Anthony Caro:*
Can Company Tablet, 1975

A wide variety of clays can be used, from porcelain to a rough and groggy mixture. Either you use a clay which has the right character for the objects you are making, or you fit the objects to the quality of the clay. 'Slabbing bodies' (clay for making slab pots) need not be so plastic and therefore shrink less than throwing bodies. Currently I use a mixture of 3 parts ball clay, 1 part fireclay and 2 parts saggar clay, which I fire to 1280°–1300°C in a reduction atmosphere.

If you are firing in an oxidised atmosphere this gives you the chance of a wider range of coloured bodies which will not need glazing. You need a refractory body to which to add coloured oxides because they are strong fluxes and bring down the 'bloating' or blistering temperature of your clay. Between 2 per cent and 4 per cent of manganese dioxide (giving grey brown when fired) or copper oxide (making soft green), kneaded into a plastic body, gives good results. It is worth trying most of the common colouring oxides and other materials, such as 10 per cent wood ash which gives the body a toasty look, or others, such as sawdust, cork or sand for texture. The proportions suggested are based on the weight of plastic clay and oxides or ash weighed dry.

It is quicker to cut slabs from a block than to roll them out individually. Try the clay a bit harder than throwing consistency. Wedge it thoroughly and beat it into a block, the top of which is the size of the largest slab you will need.

There are a great many tools for cutting the block into slabs. My way is fairly simple and cheap, but it does require a little practice – your first slabs will probably be uneven. I use two strands of wire about 50cm long twisted together and with toggled ends. This gives the slabs a finely corrugated surface. The wire is stretched between two grooved sticks and drawn through just below the top of the clay block. The wire is then lowered a slab thickness and drawn through again and again until you reach the bottom.

The two sticks can be easily made in half an hour. They should be about 30×2.5×2.5cm (12″×1″×1″). At one end, cut grooves with a saw to produce 6mm (¼″) slabs, and at the other end 8mm (⅓″) slabs, as illustrated. By missing out a groove when cutting the clay you can double the

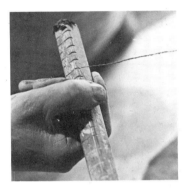

Using a twisted wire and guide sticks cut slabs from a block

Slab-building

thickness of the slab. If you mark numbers against the grooves it is easier to make sure that you have the wire at the same level on each stick.

The top and bottom slabs are not used. The rest are carefully picked up to avoid leaving finger marks and laid out on boards. (Newspaper will prevent the clay sticking to the board.) We want these slabs to dry out until they bend very little under their own weight. Turn the slabs over half way through the drying to stop them curling up.

You will probably find it is quite difficult to get slabs to dry out and then make something from them in the same day. They need to dry fairly slowly to keep them of an even hardness. If you stack them back together when leather-hard and totally wrap them in plastic they will keep for weeks, provided the wrapping is done very thoroughly.

To build slab pots you need a few simple tools. I cut my shapes out with a paint stripper. I buy the thinnest 7.5cm (3") steel variety and sharpen up both the sides with a file, so turning it into a broad-bladed knife which guides itself very efficiently through the clay. Make your first project a simple four-sided form with a base.

The slab-builder's tools

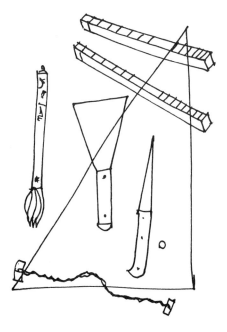

Cutting the slabs and, below, preparing the joint

You will need a large plastic set-square if you want the sides to be rectangular (this also gives you a straight edge) and a sharp pointed tool to scratch the slabs for joining, a bushy brush and water.

Cut out four sides and scratch all surfaces to be joined. We are going to assemble these with two slabs inside and two outside – see pictures. If you hold the knife almost flat to the clay you will ruck up more clay with less scratching. Brush

water on to the scratching. This will make the clay disintegrate to a thin surface of slurry. Press joints together. By squeezing both sides of the pot along the joints we can thoroughly weld two joints at the same time. I sometimes put the pot on its side and lightly beat the slabs together with a piece of wood. This can also give a textured surface.

Cut out the base a little too large; scratch, water and join to the sides and beat on. Chop off the surplus with the paint stripper.

It is quite a good idea to let this newly assembled piece dry out a while before fettling. I quite often use my stripper or a Surform blade for this. It

Having painted the joints with water, the box is assembled and the joints firmed up two at a time, as shown top right. When the base has been added and trimmed to size, the box is fettled with a Surform blade, as shown right.

97

By crinkling up thin slabs you can join them when leather-hard to make interlocking forms.

depends what kind of surface you are after. It really pays to spend quite a good deal of time and care working on this, as you can completely transform the whole feel of a piece. Make a single pot to get the technique, but after that you might find it is a good idea to make up enough slabs for three or four pieces and assemble them all. By the time you have completed the last, the first will be ready for fettling.

Slab thickness

Find out what different thickness of slabs can do for you. Try 4mm (⅛″) or 2.5cm (1″). I have found that the very thin slabs can be crinkled up in wave patterns when plastic, left to get leather-hard, then several slabs can be joined together. The thicker ones enable you to make very solid-looking shapes or ones that can be deeply carved. Thin slabs can be used for making quite large forms even when heavily pierced by holes, if you strengthen them with clay struts made from the strips left over when cutting out the sides. Two-centimetre strips of clay at intervals can make thin slabs quite rigid and easily assembled. This also cuts down warping considerably.

Silhouettes and proportions

The silhouette of a piece is very important; quite often it is this that registers first. It can be as simple as a cornflakes packet or as complicated as a combine harvester but if it is not properly thought out it really hits you over the head. I do not think there are such things as good proportions. I do not believe in the golden measure. Provided you get the details right you can get any set of sizes to work. Everything from the proportions down to the texture, the quality of edge colour, etc. must work together – but then, of course, I could find these relationships pleasing and you could hate them!

Most forms have two broad elements. Firstly, a realistic or abstract idea and secondly, technique. Just as throwing is likely to give us circular forms, so a form built from slabs is likely to be box-like and have flat or gently curved surfaces. A slabbed bird will look different from a bird made from thrown bits. Thus the

Islamic tower by Bryan Newman

By piercing a block of clay as shown opposite, before cutting, windows appear when the slabs are sliced. Clay struts added to the inside give strength before making a construction like the block of flats right.

Fruit bowl from soft slabs, by Tony Birks

areas: the boat becomes a wind-bent tree or a bridge. Sometimes an element of a completed piece becomes the next idea, crosses which started out as the superstructure of a slab-built boat become the bishop in a chess set or people on a crowded landscape.

Quite often you can get a different slant by using forms or techniques derived from other crafts, metalwork, dressmaking, cookery, etc. You do not have to be too literal in the translation. Dovetailing or riveting can become the source for a new form or decoration. Dressmaking could provide you with the idea of a form covered by a thin outer layer buttoned or draped on, part revealing, part hiding what is underneath.

There are both negative and positive aspects to the copying of ideas and techniques. So much has been said about its debit side that we are in danger of forgetting the credit. It is quite a useful way of getting things started, and often in the

technique will strongly affect the feel of the piece.

Ideas are sorted out to a great extent by the technique. So a slab boat is much more easy to see working than a slab flower, though it might be fun to try!

Forming your thoughts into forms

The elements of painting are not very far away from our slab box. The box can quite easily be flattened, to present us with two large rectangular surfaces crying out to be filled in, or the box can turn into a base to be built on, or elaborated into a sculptural form. Try building in clay the very first thing you see or think of, or some everyday object, be it telephone, train or tadpole. The first ones could look quite like our familiar telephone, but then we might begin to concentrate on the two interlocking forms of the handset and the body. Sometimes by turning an idea sideways or upside-down we get into new

The arched hull of a boat turns into a bridge.

Slab box by Ian Auld

process of copying shapes comes an understanding of the underlying principles behind forms and techniques, and this can be a useful foundation on which to build. Remember that if you have one idea, you have one idea, but if you have two you really have three because you can join the two together. Likewise, with three ideas you can come up with six permutations.

Glazing

You need to find glazes which suit the character of your work, though a simple box is quite neutral and could take any glaze from dry to shiny. I found that shiny glazes which might enhance undulating forms looked terrible on the cut edges of my sculpture.

Try these simple recipes as starting points for a wide range of ash glazes. I fire them in a reduced atmosphere at 1280°–1300°C, but they are also usable in electric kilns with an oxidising atmosphere.

Below: Kwakiutl wooden bowl from British Columbia, with semi-figurative carving

Slab-building

1 Wood ash   3
  Potash felspar   3
  (Shiny, clear, heavily crazed)

2 Wood ash   3
  Potash felspar   3
  China clay   2
  (Matt opaque buff, brown where thin)

3 Wood ash   50
  Ball clay   50
  Iron oxide   2
  (Semi-matt, runny)

4 Wood ash   40
  China clay   50
  (Apply very thinly. Dry buff breaking yellow.)

By adding ¼ per cent–3 per cent of colouring oxides you can get a wide range of colours.

5 One other dry surface I have found very useful is:
  Potash felspar   20
  Whiting   40
  China clay   50–80
  Borocalcite   2
  Yellow ochre   3
  (Apply very thinly. Buff breaking red. Try putting this glaze over Nos 2 and 3.)

Preparing ash

Being essentially a lazy person, I simplified the method of preparing ash that I had been taught. Any wood or plant ash can be used. It is amazing how much wood is needed to produce ash in quantity. A whole apple tree only produces a small tubful. It is likely that you will obtain yours from a wood-burning grate or bonfire. I burn my ash (usually apple-tree ash) on a corrugated iron base to keep it way from earth, which spoils it. I take most of the charcoal out with a 6mm (¼") mesh sieve and bag up the fine grey powder ready for making into glazes. It still has a fair amount of rubbish in it, but provided you use ash with the same amount of rubbish for the test and glaze batch you should get similar results.

I weigh up my glaze formula: say, 1 lb of ash and 1 lb of china clay, add water and put it through an 80 mesh sieve. This gets rid of the rubbish. I do not bother with washing out the soluble alkali as with my simple mixture it does not make much difference. If you want to wash the ash, the time to do it is when it has been made up into a glaze. Simply allow the fine parts to settle, pour off the water, add fresh water and stir, repeating the process five to ten times.

Firing

Sometimes it is quite difficult to pick up finished work to load into the kiln for biscuit firing without breaking it. I overcome this by building on the kiln shelf.

Some of my sculptures have legs. The glazed legs would stick to the kiln shelf and the shrinkage in firing would cause distortion. I overcome this by firing the piece on a slab of raw clay through the biscuit and on the same slab through the glaze firing. I brush a little refractory sand mixed in water on the bottom of the legs to stop them sticking to the clay slab.

Conclusion

The ways of translating an idea into clay, or the ability to see the possibilities of a clay technique can take quite some time to develop. Lots of projects will only be half successful but as long as you go at them with the attitude: 'I am going to discover something from this,' rather than 'Look what a mess I have made,' all will be well.

*Top: bowl by Jane Waller, 20cm in diameter, made by combining clays as described on page 107.
Right: pinch-built bowl by Ruth Duckworth, with rising central form glazed with porcelain ash glaze as described on page 72.*

13
Combined clay techniques

There is no helpful umbrella word for the kind of pottery which depends on the contrasts between different colours of clay body within a single piece. Agateware, clay mosaic, neriage, scroddled ware are some of the names given to its many branches. It certainly lies astride pottery making and pottery decoration, for the decoration is indeed in the making and the fabric of the pots.

Clay body can be coloured by wedging in metal oxides or prepared body stain, and all the pots described here are made by putting such modified clays together with uncoloured clay and *not* wedging it together.

If the pot is not to fall apart, it is important that pots made from clays of different colours should have the same basic composition. Unfortunately metal oxides in large quantities – over 5 per cent of the dry weight – affect the shrinkage and certainly increase the likelihood of bloating or blistering. At the boundary between the coloured and the uncoloured clay adhesion is often poor, and this is where such pots may break up, especially at high temperatures. A beginner is advised, therefore, to fire combined clay pots at earthenware temperatures, and not to mix different bodies, which only adds to the problem.

Start with a white clay, such as 'T' Material or a fine white earthenware body and wedge it up.

Over 50cm high, this handsome coiled pot by Ewen Henderson has a pattern which comes from mixing white clay with dark in the pads of clay he uses for pot making.

Then put half of it away under a polythene cover and wedge into the balance a mixture of strong colouring oxide. Iron is well-behaved, and cobalt and copper are good but strong. Manganese is helpful in small quantities but is inclined to make the clay 'flux' and go runny if too liberally used. Mixing equal quantities of all four, totalling 7½ per cent of the clay's dry weight, produces a dark, slatey-blue, showing the dominance of cobalt oxide over the others. For a brighter colour, use cobalt alone at 5 per cent of the dry weight. For a warmer colour use iron with a pinch of manganese.

Make sure the oxides are finely ground like black flour before sprinkling them into the clay and kneading. It is a messy business, and cleanliness is all. When you have kneaded the stained clay to an even, dark grey, wrap this up too, and clean everything around, from the workbench to your own hands. Stray bits of colourant contaminating the white clay will progressively reduce the impact of your work, which depends upon contrast.

The need for clean surfaces precludes the use of grog or powdered clay to aid in the rolling out of slabs from the two clays, and the best surface to use in these circumstances is slate or plaster. Roll out some slabs of white clay first, and then, having cleaned the rolling pin, similar-sized slabs of coloured clay. Without waiting for them to dry, make a multi-decker sandwich of alternate layers. Press down on the pile, and using a straight edge and sharp knife cut vertically through the sandwich, revealing a liquorice-all-sorts type pattern in the slice. If

Combined clay techniques

numerous vertical sections are cut each about 6mm thick, you have the basis for a patterned pot, either slab-built or moulded.

Small 'tiles' of striped clay units about 2.5cm square are convenient. These can be pressed firmly together in a shallow mould, or over a hump mould, or even the outside profile of another pot. It is essential to use no water, and to keep the fingertips clean, or the hard edges of colour change will be blurred by the pressure of the fingers. It is nevertheless important to apply this pressure or the clay pieces will not be adequately bonded together.

If the striped slabs of clay are themselves stacked in a pile, preferably 'out of phase', and again cut vertically in slices, a chequered pattern will emerge which can be similarly used or can form the basis of slab pots. The joining of the slab surfaces must be done with the minimum of slurry, or again the pattern will be blurred. Precise patterns or representational designs can be made by this means, but much is to be said for assembling the pattern block at random, just as variegated brick walls or tiled floors look best if the builder has taken his material randomly from the pile.

Alternating layers of different coloured clays will make a striped sandwich when cut into strips. The strips can be chopped into rectangular blocks and used as units of pattern.

The results of arranging the clay carefully can be as varied at the patterns through seaside rock.

Chequer boxes by the author

Often the action of cutting through the clay with the knife will create a curving or wavy line, not unlike the feathering patterns in slip, and it is sensible to use this in the design rather than to try to prevent it.

One precise technique has been perfected by Jane Waller, in conjunction with press-moulds. To prevent the plaster from absorbing too much of the clay's moisture, she paints the mould's surface with shellac and then oils it lightly with motor oil. She then arranges balls of clay of several different colours, each ball the size of a chick-pea, over the surface of the mould, and presses them carefully but firmly against the wall of the mould with a pestle covered in linseed oil soaked cotton cloth. By holding the pestle at right angles to the mould's surface and keeping a regular pressure, this creates the hexagonal honeycomb pattern which always results when round things are pressed closely together, and the linseed oil prevents the different clays from getting smeared. By choosing the clay colours carefully and glazing only very lightly to keep the heightened tactile quality of the pot itself, the result can be most beautiful, as the colour photograph on page 103 shows.

By making small rosettes of unblended clays, preferably using several colours, Jane Waller's technique can be adapted to make millefiori patterns under a clear, shiny glaze, like the popular glass paperweights which bear this name.

Only by rhythmically kneading the clay can the colours we have been at such pains to keep apart be made to disappear and blend totally. At intermediate stages when the cross-section of the clay shows no formal pattern, it can be used to press mould agateware, such as the cats by Andrew Lord shown overleaf. Agateware, which can also be made using the slab-building technique, has recently regained popularity, and often looks better if several colours of clay are mixed – perhaps dark green, dark blue and white. By splitting a slab of agate clay into two and exposing both faces side by side, patterns like matching veneers on furniture are created, although this technique has never had much appeal for me.

Combined clay techniques are not confined to moulded or slabbed ware. They can also be used in throwing. By putting different coloured clays together unmixed in a single lump on the wheel head, distinct spiral patterns are automatically produced up the sides of the pots thrown. For the colour changes to be clear-cut it is important to throw almost without water. The

Combined clay techniques

Press-moulded agate cats by Andrew Lord

Striated plate, 60cm wide, by Ruth Duckworth

range of shapes this sort of pattern suits is limited, but it can be graceful, as on the pot by Marianne de Trey shown right.

In Japan, potters cut grooves in partly thrown pots and inlay coloured clay strips made by slicing a coil down the middle. They then continue throwing and the clear-cut pattern emerges. The type of pattern depends on the angle at which the inlaid clay is placed, but there is always a spiral tendency, which indicates, by the way, the direction of movement of particles within the plastic clay when it is being shaped on the wheel.

By arranging coils or small slabs of clay of a single colour in a pattern or representational design on a hump mould, a more pictorial decoration than those achieved by the various processes described above can be made when this pattern is overlaid with a sheet of clay of contrasting colour and the two combined with pressure from a rolling pin. These patterns are always somewhat distorted, and therefore too detailed a scheme should not be attempted. At the same time the junction between the two clays is always distinctive and well-preserved using this method.

Spiral-pattern bowl by Marianne de Trey

The combined-clays method of integral decoration can be used with slip-casting; agate patterns on the surface of cast pots are easy to make by using different coloured slips and swirling them about whilst still wet. A dark slip squeezed on to the walls of a plaster mould and allowed to harden somewhat before adding either plastic clay or casting slips will produce a hard-edge pattern which can be quite intricate.

By applying dots of oxide-stained slip to the wall of the plaster mould just before pouring in the slip, a coloured pattern is inlaid into the cast.

Combined clay techniques

The delicate porcelain bowl by Jacqueline Poncelet, illustrated on the right, was made in this way.

Some of the pinched ware of Mary Rogers, described and illustrated in Chapter 10, uses contrasting clays to good effect, and most of these techniques can be practised by the potter at home, since the normal facilities of a pottery are not required, and the kind of pot produced is usually small in scale. Combined clay techniques provide one of the growth points for contemporary ceramics and all readers of this book are encouraged to try.

Above and top right: porcelain bowls by Jacqueline Poncelet decorated with coloured casting slips.

14 Extruding

A toothpaste tube is an extruder, and as children and toothpaste manufacturers know the toothpaste can be made more interesting by varying the form of the nozzle. In principle, plastic material is forced under controlled pressure through a hole. Apart from those slip trailers, which are described in Chapter 16, used for extruding liquid clay from a fine nozzle to make patterns, extruders are not normally regarded as amongst the potter's tools. Brickworks or drainpipe manufacturers rely upon them and in industry some of the coarser hardware of the firing process is extruded, using a primitive 'wad mill'.

A hand extruder using the leverage principle, as illustrated below, is a spectacular but simple

tool of great interest, particularly to the sculptural potter. Well-prepared clay is simply pressed through a die at the bottom of the cylinder and by the insertion of a centre to this die on a strong steel spider, hollow forms can be extruded with precision and a minimum of effort.

'Isn't it rather like cheating?' commented one of my pupils, whose hard-learned throwing skills seemed suddenly superfluous when I demonstrated how easily an extruder would produce long cylinders, box-section ceramics, or simply long, perfect rods of clay according to the shape of the die. Of course the extrusion,

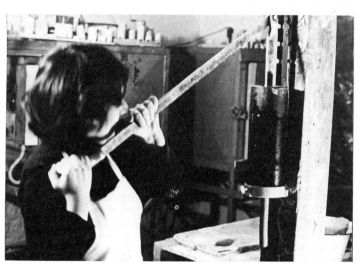

A metal die is screwed firmly into place at the bottom of the extrusion tube. A block of clay is placed inside, and the lever pulled down to press *the clay out through the die. A long lever exerts great pressure, and the extruder must be firmly fixed to the wall.*

Traditionally, ribbed extruded handles have been used for jugs and similar large pots, as shown on page 120, and they have a specially energetic 'spring', quite unlike that of moulded handles, though they are less natural looking than pulled handles. It is the energy of the extrusion which makes it especially interesting, both when adapted for use with functional pots, such as the handles described above, or used in sculptural pieces. Long, straight or tensely curved forms give the sculptural potter the opportunity of building taller, thinner, finer pots than by any other method outside the much more laborious process of casting. The materials for extrusion can vary from heavily grogged fireclay to white porcelain, and the results seem to emphasise both the rigidity and the pliability of clay. It is important not to succumb to the tyranny of hard-edged extruded forms, but to remember that whilst soft these can be bent, intertwined, attenuated and perforated. The pictures show some of the sculptural work made with the help of a simple hand extruder, and the photographs alongside show how hollow extrusions are made. It is necessary to have a very strong fixing point on a wall, as the leverage principle allows heavy pressure to be brought to bear on the clay.

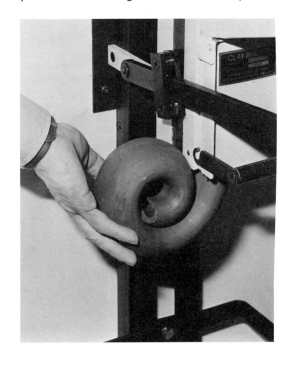

The top picture shows the spider which allows hollow extrusions to be made, like the square-sectioned box form above. They can be straight or curved by hand as they come out.

whatever its shape, is not a substitute for a thrown or slab-built ceramic, for it has a totally different feel and character. I would not recommend using extruded rods as substitute coils for coiled pots, nor flat-sectioned extrusions for slabware. As the clay passes through the die it is given an unmistakable 'untouched by hand' finish and the potter must use this to his advantage, or not use it at all.

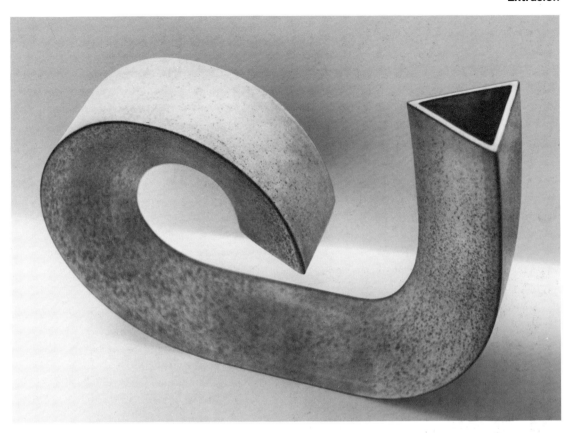

Extruded sculptural forms

Most pottery suppliers now list extruders, sometimes called bulleys, though the old-fashioned screw-down wad mill type should be avoided (see page 133 for details).

Section Three - Pattern, Surface and Design

15 Tiles

The tile panel is essentially a flat ceramic surface for decorative or practical purposes. Many potters prefer to buy ready-made plain tiles

Medieval inlay tile from Dorchester Friary

Left: a hand tile-cutter in use

rather than to wrestle with the problems of making their own. However, a mystique has grown up around the hand-making of tiles which is quite unnecessary, since they are very easy to make provided they are not too thin and not too large. The problems are all associated with warping. These are minimised by using a not very plastic clay with plenty of grog in it and rolling it out into flat sheets when it is much harder than would be used for slab-building. The sheets should be cut up into small units – a 15cm square is a sensible maximum size, and 10cm square is a most practical size. The tiles should not be less than 1cm thick.

A large area of clay can be incised, inlaid with slip or decorated in other ways and then cut up with a metal straight-edge or sharp knife into tiles to dry. The fired result can be re-assembled to make a single design. Plain tiles can be cut from slabs using simple cutters of the type illustrated. The drying of the tiles should be very slow, and they are best piled one on top of another so that their edges cannot easily curl up. Turning the tiles over once or twice during the drying will help to keep them from warping, and they can be scraped and fettled and even sandpapered when they are bone-dry. The edges are important. Most commercial tiles

have a 'cushion' edge, which prevents people from cutting their hands when washing around the sink. It is good to avoid really sharp edges, especially as once laid down, tiles are likely to be grouted between the join, so you can round the upper edges of each tile with sandpaper if you wish.

Making the 64 units of a chess board is a satisfying exercise in ceramics. It need take no more than an evening to prepare the pieces, and another evening to glaze half of them a dark colour and the other half light. The result when set into a wooden panel will be a heavy board to carry around, but a very attractive playing surface, and it is especially appropriate if set into the top of a table. Floor tiles or fireplace surrounds can easily be undertaken provided that a uniform result is not expected. It is pointless for the studio potter to try to compete with commercial producers in making smooth and plain tiles, but small batches, if all fired together in the same kiln, will have individuality as well as a family likeness. Cutting interlocking shapes is quite feasible provided the forms are kept simple.

Only small tiles should be fired to stoneware temperatures, since warping in the kiln is much more likely above 1200°C.

Painted tile panel by Maggie Berkowitz

The potential for glazing and decorating huge flat areas is enormous, as many painters like Matisse discovered for themselves.

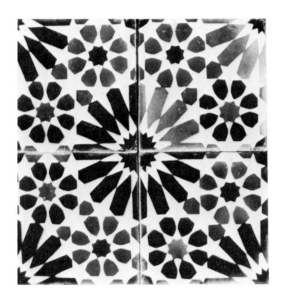

Do not forget that the arrangement of identical tiles allows the build up of pattern motifs larger than the individual unit. The traditional design shown left is a good example, well suited to silk-screen or stencilled application.

16 Decoration

The decoration of pottery is a subject for a book in itself – or several books. How can it all be described in a single chapter? The answer is that it cannot, any more than throwing can be. But whilst throwing can be learned comfortably in a lifetime, decoration and ornament is something broader, too massive to be learned or experienced by a single artist. The potter can only follow his own inclinations, and try some of the many techniques, old and new.

Decoration made by winding tape around tall shapes before spraying. Pots by Val Barry.

In an attempt to be fairly comprehensive, in this chapter a great number of decorative techniques will be described briefly, with illustrations. It cannot be complete, or even tidy, for decoration spills over the boundary of pottery into sculpture, painting, calligraphy and lithography. Is a clay-and-enamel roadsign 'Acacia Avenue' decorated pottery? Should a Roman mosaic made of multi-coloured clay tessarae be called pottery? Each uses a pottery decorating technique, and many of these merge or overlap with techniques already described – the use of slip, glazing, texturing with tools. It is incorrect to say: 'think of the decoration as part of the pot, to keep the unity both in approach and finished result,' for this would exclude dishes used as vehicles for painted or silk-screened design. It is helpful, however, to think of the finished result when making the pot. You may decide that a simple, plain glaze is quite enough decoration for the form you are making – or you may start decorating from the moment you roll out the clay . . .

Some decoration starts with the texture of the clay. Wedging coarse grog or sand into clay makes it scratchy – a scratchiness revealed if you scrape the surface or plane it with a Surform tool or a cheese grater. Now try wedging something coarser into the clay: granulated cork, rice grains, tapioca, tea-leaves . . . very coarse additions will make the clay painful to throw, or simply prevent it from being plastic enough for throwing. This does not stop it from being used for press-moulds or slabs. Vegetable matter like straw fires away in the kiln, leaving a pumice-like texture. It is decorative in itself and its decorative possibilities are enhanced when it is glazed, especially if the clay is stained with colourants, sponged on.

Clay can be decoratively textured when the pot is made, or half-made. Tool texturing is customary with coiled pots, and slabs can be impressed with designs before or during construction. Avoid 'automatic' textures, like the rough side of hardboard or the patterns given by woven materials, which look particularly dead on pottery. Remember that you can 'draw' on plastic clay, as Picasso did, with a fine point or needle – a drawing which can be made to stand out at a later stage by squeezing colourant into the cracks. The same tool, or a ball-point pen, a turning tool or wooden stick, can be used to make regular lines or random patterns, and the quality of the line depends partly on the state of the clay. The small press-moulded pot by Jane Waller (see page 47) was given a deep, serrated pattern before pressing by using a lino-cutter to cut into leather-hard clay.

A simple cork roulette, its pattern, and the effect of subsequent rolling

Some textural patterns are unsuitable for domestic ware – they can have sharp edges or create dust-traps. If you do put deep patterns on household pots, make sure it is somewhere it does not upset function: on the outside of storage jars, for example. Pottery suppliers sell rollers or 'roulettes' which impress patterns across clay much as pastry rollers do. Essentially, the pattern must repeat itself, and a simple roller can be made from a cork cut with a knife. Old wooden printing blocks are popular instruments for pressing letters into pottery. Letters can be carved into plastic clay with a sharp blade, but beginners often make a mess of this: letter-carving needs specialised training and, in any case, I always find inscriptions around pots rather tiresome, as one has to turn the pot like Trajan's column to get the full story.

A plunge pot with pumice-stone texture left after the burning away of cork fragments wedged into the clay.

Decoration

Texture from tools

Automatic pattern-makers, like the ends of turning tools or seger cones, make a routine appearance when students are casting around for something to use and the results are not always what you would expect. It is worth trying all the objects in your work-room, from knives to bottle tops, as a means of pressing a design on plastic clay. Personal seals for impressing can be carved on the ends of plaster of Paris plugs and are often used by potters as their 'signature' on the bottom or side of a pot.

Before leaving the subject of impressed design, it is worth mentioning that patterns made in this way can be modified interestingly by rolling the clay with a rolling pin *after* the impression.

Fluted ware

There is a tradition in the East of carving into thrown pottery in a way which is similar to bas-relief sculpture. A bowl will have a part of its surface left thick by the thrower so that some of the clay can later be carved away when this pot has gone beyond the leather-hard stage. The greenish celadon glazes of China show up this carving very sensitively. It is also traditional to flute the sides of a thrown pot, using a bamboo fluting tool (obtainable from most ceramic suppliers) or simply by using a bow of strong wire attached to a wooden handle. The shape of the wire will, of course, affect the shape of the fluting, and the potter can decide whether to make it straight up and down or spiral.

Very thickly thrown pots can, when they have hardened a little, be faceted into polygons by slicing down through the clay with a knife or cutting wire.

Cutting right through

The kind of mark which a knife makes through clay depends partly on the knife and partly on how hard the clay is. If it is soft and squashy, the marks can be quite nice, but if it is too hard and chalky they will certainly be unpleasant. If you have the time, get a thrown bowl or slab pot and cut bits out of it periodically as it dries. In that way you will find out exactly the best stage at which to carve the pot.

Fluted pot by Lucie Rie

There has been a fashion recently for making perforated pots – cutting holes in the walls of thrown bowls or slip-cast bowls, and the results can be quite arbitrary. You cannot expect a good design to happen naturally or accidentally. Unless you plan the perforated decoration it will probably look silly. At the same time, cut clay, especially porcelain, can look extremely beautiful, as the translucent porcelain of Jacqueline Poncelet shows.

Adding clay

Instead of cutting the clay away, you can add it, simply pressing soft or softened clay surfaces together, either as seals or as strips on the side of thrown pots (see Chapter 9) or thin ribs on to pinched bowls (see Chapter 10), or free-standing shapes on to sculptural pots (see Chapter 12). Handles and lugs, of course, come into this category and at times past have been the principal decorative feature of pots. Some potters create decorative handles very

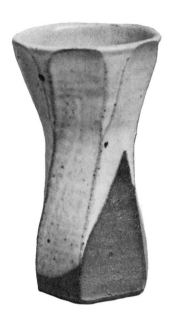

Faceted pot by Marianne de Trey

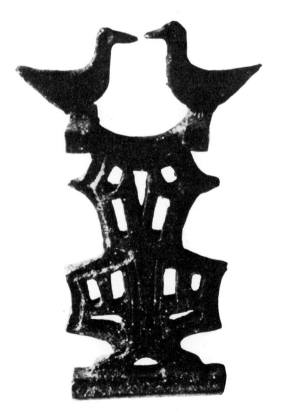

A strong design in cut clay by David Edmonds

A porcelain bowl perforated and finely carved by Jacqueline Poncelet

Decoration

imaginatively, as shown in folk pottery in all parts of the world.

Added clay should be of the same consistency if possible as the body of the pot, although it may be coloured differently. One of the most formal traditional ways of adding clay is by 'sprigging'. In this technique, shown in the English folk-art teapot below, plastic clay (or porcelain 'paste') is first pressed into small plaster moulds where it quickly dries to a state which is handleable and then attached to the side of the pot with a little slip. Usually, but not always, the design stands out from the body of the pot because of the colour contrast with the body. Wedgwood Jasper ware is the best-known example and the technique seems to suit a wide range of shapes.

Slipping and inlay

Say 'slip' and dozens of new methods of decoration open up before you. My own favourite is inlay. This is achieved by carving a design into the body of the pot, painting a very thick slip of contrasting colour over the carved

Tree-fellers make the handles on this vessel by Christine Poole, while applied decoration makes a bird in its nest.

area, and when the slip has dried, scraping away the surplus to show the engraved design in its original detail. When the colour contrast is strong, the effect is to emphasise the carved design, and it can be used on all kinds of pottery. It is a very practical way of decorating tiles, especially floor tiles, as shown by the medieval tile on page 114, and highly suitable for dishes cast from hump moulds as the final surface of the interior will be smooth.

Slip can be put all over the surface of a leather-hard pot and decoration created by scratching or wiping through to the body clay below. A sponge or finger must be used boldly while the slip is still wet to make a design which looks deliberate. If you wait till the slip is dry, or at least as dry as the body of the pot below, the design has to be scratched through with a pin or wooden modelling tool. Try various tools with the aim of removing the slip layer neatly, without unduly carving into the body below. Many magnificent pots have been made in this way, especially in the Middle East, but

An English folk art teapot with sprigged decoration and an extruded handle

Right: a bold design scratched through slip on a platter by David Smith. Below: decoration both applied and incised on a jar by Bernard Leach.

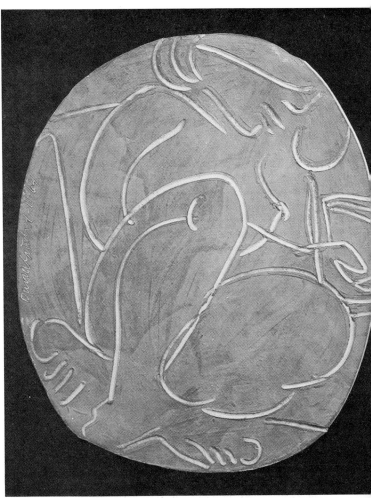

Below: incising a design which can be inlaid with slip in a press-moulded dish.

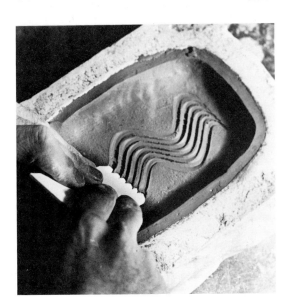

beginners often do fiddly designs, and this sgraffito technique has not the vigour of painting.

Anyone unsure of himself who wants to use the contrast between dark and light slip is advised to try paper patterns. This method is highly recommended, for it allows bold and deliberate design, and although it is slow it is very reliable. To decorate a shallow bowl by this method, cut with scissors a piece of strong newspaper into the shape you want (the patterns made by folding and cutting are good) and slightly dampen the newspaper before sticking it against the leather-hard clay of the bowl. When it is finally fixed you can pour slip over the whole of the bowl and later, when the slip has dried to a matt state, peel away the paper.

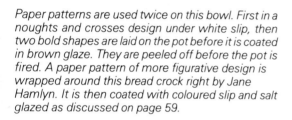

Paper patterns are used twice on this bowl. First in a noughts and crosses design under white slip, then two bold shapes are laid on the pot before it is coated in brown glaze. They are peeled off before the pot is fired. A paper pattern of more figurative design is wrapped around this bread crock right by Jane Hamlyn. It is then coated with coloured slip and salt glazed as discussed on page 59.

A surprisingly popular, but more difficult technique, is wax resist, which – like lithography and silk-screen printing – depends on the antipathy between water-based liquids like glazes and slip, and oily substances like a mixture of turpentine and candlewax. If you use these two last materials in about equal quantities, they should be heated up in a tin sitting in a pan of hot water, and the resulting liquid must be kept hot and runny until it is painted on to a leather-hard pot with an old brush. Choose a simple design. A great many things can go wrong: the pot can be too dry, so that the painted wax curls up and falls off, the paintbrush can go hard or all the bristles can fall out, and drips of hot wax can fall on to the pot where you do not want them to be. The vital thing is to keep the pattern simple, with not too many fine lines. The wax will dry almost instantly, and when you pour or paint slip over it, the slip will shrink away from the wax, creating a strong but often spotty 'negative' of the design you have painted. The wax will burn

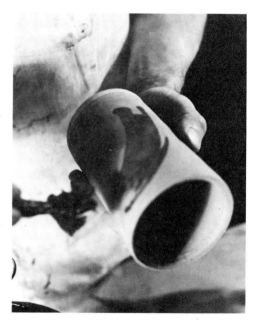

An old floppy brush, or even pieces of string, will make a bold mark in hot wax on the side of a pot. Slip or glaze poured over the design will shrink away, as shown right.

away in the kiln leaving the bare clay underneath. This technique needs a good deal of practice and flair for the impromptu pattern. The same technique with glaze was used with consummate skill by Shoji Hamada in decorating the pot shown on page 69.

Trailing

Liquid slip can be used as a drawing medium by extruding it through a nozzle attached to a little rubber bag. The great slip-masters of the seventeenth century probably used bladders, and many potters today use a rubber bulb with a nozzle. I personally prefer to use a very thick-gauge polythene bag attached to a glass nozzle, so that I can see the slip as I squeeze it out. The technique is like icing a cake. The thickness of the slip is vital – if it is too runny it will spread out too much to be an effective drawing line. If it is too hard it will crack away from the body clay. Mix the slip by adding clay and water and oxide colourant, if required, until it is like thick cream, and sieve it well to make sure that it is absolutely smooth.

It is very important to practise on scraps of clay slab before you try to 'ice' your pot, and if you have difficulty in drawing freely, restrict your efforts to a symmetrical pattern of lines – or lines and spots. Slip trailing these simple patterns is easy. Creative decoration using a slip trailer can be marvellous, but it is difficult and there is no going back once you have started.

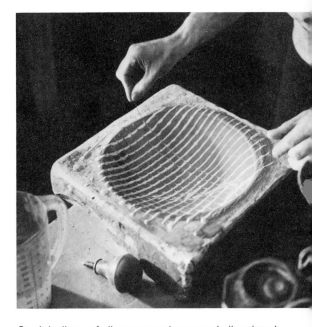

Straight lines of slip squeezed on to a shallow bowl, then 'feathered' by drawing a bristle from a stiff brush through the wet surface at right angles to the lines.

Decoration

The most commonly used slip for trailing is white, often on a ground of plain brown or black slip over a red clay base. This is unfortunate, since white slip tends to crack away more readily than other colours, and the design can be lost or at least spoiled. It is more sensible to use a coloured slip on a white ground, if it suits your purpose.

Painting

All the techniques of decoration described so far have been applied before the pot is fired, either on to plastic or leather-hard clay. Not much can be done to a bone-hard pot, apart from the tidying processes and painting with a brush.

Painting is more frequently used for decoration on a biscuit-fired pot under or on the glaze, but it can be used for decoration at any stage after the shaping process. The feel of the brush full of slip or oxide stain on an unfired pot changes as the pot surface dries. A bone-dry clay pot plucks at the brush, just as a biscuit-fired pot does. In fact

Some of the pottery decorator's tools. Below: bowl with painted lustre decoration by Alan Caiger-Smith.

Right: hard-edge decoration on a Pueblo Indian pot. Below: geometrical decoration on handmade tiles arranged in a bold pattern.

it is only when the clay is still pretty wet that painting on pottery resembles painting on anything else. The rest of the time it is like painting on blotting-paper. If you want to paint a fairly precise design on ceramics, it is quite a good idea to try it out on blotting-paper first. Fine brushes do not hold enough liquid to travel far on absorbent surfaces, and it is certain that you will always need a larger brush for ceramic painting than you expect.

Although the blotting-paper exercise may be helpful to give you the feel of the surface, nothing but experience can help you with the thickness of colour and its intensity, for most colours in pottery are either black or brown before they are fired in the kiln. Using them is like cooking when you have a cold, rehearsing an orchestra with ear-plugs in. There is no feedback till you have something out of the kiln to tell you whether you have painted on too much or too little. Like painting a watercolour, you are likely to make a mess if you try to repaint or re-touch an unsatisfactory area, for every brush mark shows. My advice to those who want to paint on a pot before it is fired is to use a

125

Decoration

bold design, to avoid handling the pot in order to keep this design smudge-free, and to use oxides with water and a little Polycel or gum arabic to stop the paint flaking.

Decoration with the glaze

Although there are many techniques for decorating an unfired pot, it is more usual for the decoration to be done together with the glazing, after the first firing, and here painted decoration comes into its own. The surfaces are still porous like blotting-paper, however, whether the brush-painting is done before or after the glaze coat is applied.

The colour of the chosen glaze is important to the decoration, of course, and certain glazes, particularly the dark brown/black glaze known as tenmoku, have a happy knack of changing colour where there is a change of angle on the pot's side, and no further decoration is required.

The overlapping of glazes can give powerful decorative effects, as can leaving certain parts of pots bare during the dipping process. Provided the position of the bare midriff is chosen with care, this can be as positive a feature of decoration as putting a belt on a dress.

Tenmoku glaze 'breaking' on the edges of a faceted pot by Marianne de Trey

Horizontal bands are very easily added to symmetrical thrown pots by the expedient of a banding wheel sold by ceramic suppliers or an ordinary potter's wheel (either electric or pedal) and allowing the tip of a colourant loaded brush to touch it. Provided there is plenty of liquid on the brush, a clean and even line will appear all round the pot. Such bands can be used singly as the sole decorative feature, or in pairs on either side of another design as boundaries to it. More arbitrary lines which have an energetic look are made by pouring glaze or colour from one vessel into another in a thin stream, and passing the pot to be decorated swiftly under this

Cylinders by Robin Welch, part glazed, part bare

A cylinder being decorated on a banding wheel

stream. Control of the design is minimal, but the result always looks better than a pot on to which the colour has simply been dribbled.

Repeating designs can usefully be applied to cylinders. Squashed, two-sided pots, if they need any decoration at all, look well with two panels, one on each side, and irregular shaped pots, such as jugs with lips and handles, can often be wittily decorated by incorporating the spout and handle into the decoration.

A pattern which proceeds around the pot is a useful device. Although it can be used happily around a cylinder, I think it is best practised on an open bowl shape where the whole design can be taken in at a single glance.

Narrative and striking design combined on a classic Greek bowl. The tradition is maintained by Eric Mellon, whose design below is painted on the outside of this bowl, with a peacock on the footring.

Decoration

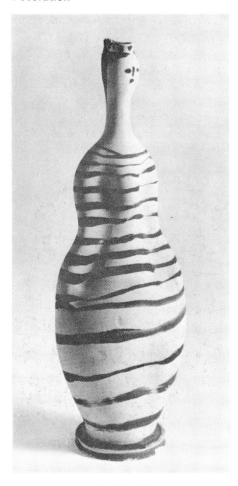

Woman with hands hidden. Modelled and slip-painted by Picasso.

Apart from combining glazes and brushing or pouring on oxide colourants, designs on biscuit or glazed pots can be done with oxide pencils and wax crayon, as offered by the suppliers listed on page 133. The former tend to produce rather weak, pastel colours, but the latter can be used to create a scratchy kind of drawing which is revealed when covered with glaze, and is quite unlike anything else.

Sgraffito, using a needle to scratch glaze away, as described for slip, is not very easy if neat pictorial results are required. The hard, fired clay underneath is inclined to make the glaze flake off, and this method, of course, exposes unglazed areas which may not be practical. Sgraffito on fired ware is more successful if a second glaze is applied to a pot which has already been through one glaze firing. In this case, scratching through a second glaze mixed

Sgraffito on top of glaze. Bowl by James Tower.

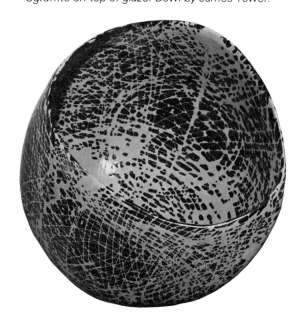

Do not try to make the repeating units too detailed or descriptive. A procession of ducks painted inside a bowl is quite likely to be disastrous, while a series of blobs in manganese made with a broad brush can be as attractive as a bowl full of plums. Remember that bowls can be decorated while turning the pot on the banding wheel; you do not need to perform contortions to decorate round the rim, and in fact this would almost certainly remove any fluency in the design. The open bowl shape has presented an intriguing challenge to designers for thousands of years and patterns which tell a narrative across the plate are amongst the most charming of Greek pots. Objects which have definite tops and bottoms – like ships and houses – are not as easy to translate on to bowls as, say, apples, birds, sweetcorn cobs or insects.

with sugar or gum arabic for adhesion will expose the glaze below, and the result can be most attractive.

Permutations of these techniques allow more possibilities than a beginner can hope to try without becoming confused, but anyone using common sense can be imaginative, and even invent their own variations, using a little ingenuity. For instance, a glaze which is known to craze will go on doing so for a period of a few hours after removal from the kiln, and if strong under-glaze colour is rubbed over the pot as soon as it is taken out of the kiln, the colour will go into the cracks. If a second contrasting colour is rubbed in an hour or so later, the new colour will stain only the *new* cracks, giving the design on the pot a remarkable three-dimensional effect when the pot is refired.

Colours vary, of course, according to their position under or on top of the glaze. Opaque glazes will soften but not obscure metal oxides, which burn through, often in attractive ways. Glazing a pot with an oxide decoration already painted on to it will, however, cause some contamination in the glaze bucket by oxide coming off the pot, and this damage to the glaze must be kept in mind. Oxides and commercial colourants painted on top of the glaze will remain bright and the wax technique described in the context of slip (page 122) can be practised on top of a glaze if the pot is handled with care. The wax-resist pattern is revealed by painting an oxide over the wax, or dipping the pot in another glaze which will shrink away just as did the slip.

Modification of a pot's decoration and surface can be carried out after it has been fired, either to redress faults or simply to make a pot more interesting. There are three decoration techniques which are carried out *only* after the first glaze firing. Enamels are extra-bright colours which are stable only at low temperatures. Consequently the glaze has to be vitrified first, and the enamels low-fired on to it. Opportunity is here for the potter who wants to paint something finicky, although it has little appeal to me.

Lustres, on the other hand, give the opportunity of a really magnificent finished surface. Pearly, iridiscent, opalescent, gold or silver lustres result from the deposit of metal salts on the pot's surface at temperatures between 750° and 1000°C, and most commercially prepared lustres mature at precisely specified temperatures. They are painted on to a pot in a

Jug with top handle and accordion player, by Christine Poole. On-glaze decoration, majolica glaze.

sticky carrier medium, and they are appropriate for detailed designs. They should be burnished after re-firing to reveal their full strength. Dipping an old toothbrush into a lustre mix (or an oxide mix for that matter) and flicking spots on to the pot's side by running a thumb over the bristles can produce a remarkable, if somewhat over-rich effect, and likewise enamels and lustres can be applied from a simple atomiser as sold by artists' suppliers for spraying pastel fixative. The kind of decoration an atomiser will offer is not necessarily as woolly as it sounds: by the use of masks, or masking tape, sharp demarcations are possible, as shown in the striped cylanders on page 116 by Val Barry. These atomiser techniques can also be used for pots which have not had their glaze firing, when the results will be more muted and the pots will look like thrushes' eggs.

Decoration

Silk-screen printing is an increasingly popular technique, since it allows the individual potter the precision of decoration which normally only comes in the factory. It can be done directly, by placing a nylon screen with shellaced pattern above the surface of the ceramic (tiles are the only pots suitable) and pressing through a mixture of ceramic pigment and an oil-based medium. Alternatively, the technique can be used indirectly by transferring the silk screen design on to a carrier film with a paper back. By floating off the paper backing the designer can transfer the design on to shapes like cylinders.

It is not sensible, or possible, to try all these decorative techniques. Remember that practice is helpful for most of them, and do not give up if your first results are disappointing.

Sgraffito and inlay design on a bowl by Lucie Rie.

17

Your own workshop

Many amateur potters dream of having a workshop of their own, and many have to settle, for want of space, for a tray and tools on the kitchen table. If you do have a room in the house or flat which is used for no other purpose, then the following information may be useful.

Potteries often get very hot, especially if the kiln is located in the workshop. The opposite can apply, however, and temperatures below freezing can have disastrous effects on glazes stored in glass jars, and on clay which is 'de-conditioned', as well as on freshly made ware which is shattered by freezing. Beware, therefore, the unheated garden shed.

The best room is a ground-floor outhouse with a source of water, drainage and heat. It will not matter if the walls of such a room are spattered with clay, and the door will probably not lead directly on to the fitted carpets of the house.

The vital item of equipment is the kiln, and how to load it, fire it and unpack it lies outside the scope of this book. It is not difficult, however, and there are several books available on kilns and on their construction. The determined beginner is best-off buying a new electric kiln. Secondhand kilns of all types are often bad buys, since the fragile used elements of electric kilns get damaged in transit, and gas and oil kilns often have to be taken apart and rebuilt. Old electric kilns are very heavy because of the fire bricks in their construction. Since about 1980, ceramic fibre insulated kilns have revolutionized kiln design, providing a high degree of insulation without great bulk.

Therefore the kiln has a relatively higher capacity or a smaller overall size and weight.

Many of these fibre kilns are loaded from the top, and they can be coupled to automatic programmers which remove both the excitement and the ordeal of waiting for a kiln to reach temperature, and having to gauge this by looking through a spyhole at a pyrometric cone which bends when it has experienced a precise amount of heat. It must be said that the huge technological advances of temperature control now allow the potter to go to bed knowing that his kiln will turn itself off during the night at the right time and using off-peak electricity. Conversion to this system has revolutionized my own life and potting.

The cost of a new fibre kiln is often less than the cost of a good motorized wheel: it is possible to equip yourself with both for under £1000, or $2000.

A tidy person can probably work in a room less than ten feet square (three metres), though I certainly could not. The kiln will take up a corner

Most needs are self-evident, or quickly learned, but to save time and frustration remember that you will really need a lot of wall hooks to hang up jugs, lawns and tools, a lot of old towels, as you need to dry your hands often, and a great many flat surfaces. If you cannot get hold of stacks with movable shelves, then wall brackets with loose boards are useful, but make sure that they are strong – jars of glaze and even unfired pots can be weighty.

However big or small your operation, keep clay in lidded bins, such as plastic dustbins, and glazes in similar bins or large-mouthed jars like sweet jars. If you keep packeted raw materials in bags on the floor, put them on wooden slats in case the floor gets wet, and above all keep plaster of Paris in a dry spot away from the clay. Do not have a carpet or mat in the room. The time will come when you will be glad that you can mop down the floor. Thermoplastic tiles are the most suitable. Pull-switches are best for electrical appliances as your hands will often be wet. Finally, no pottery room is complete without an old radio.

of the room, and will warm and dry everything which is near to it, including the potter – very helpful in winter but overwhelming in summer. At the opposite end of the room should be a cupboard with reasonably airtight doors that you can use as a damp cupboard to keep half-made ware from drying between sessions. If you are able to have a sink with hot and cold water, so much the better, otherwise you will have to carry water in buckets and bowls from elsewhere. If you have a wheel, put it under a window or in the centre of the room. It is depressing to be throwing against a wall. Likewise the solid, heavy bench you will certainly need for preparing clay is more cheerful if placed centrally, although the extra solidity provided by location against a wall may well be useful, as heavy pressure is used when kneading clay.

List of Suppliers

Most suppliers of ceramic materials issue comprehensive catalogues. These are informative, well illustrated and some of them provide a good read.

United Kingdom

Acme Marls Ltd, Bournes Bank, Burslem, Stoke-on-Trent, Staffs ST6 3DW

Cromartie Kilns, Park Hall Road, Longton, Stoke-on-Trent, Staffs ST3 5AY

Deancraft Fahey, 12 Spedding Road, Fenton Industrial Estate, Stoke-on-Trent, Staffs ST4 2ST

Dobles Fireclays, Newdowns Sand & Clay Pits, St Agnes, Cornwall

Dragon Ceramex, 5 Nomis Park, Congresbury, Avon BS19 5HB

E.C.C. Ball Clays Ltd, 36 North Street, Wareham, Dorset BH2 4AW

E.C.C. China Clays Ltd, John Keay House, St Austell, Cornwall

Fulham Pottery Ltd, 8–10 Ingate Place, London SW8 3NS

Lotus Pottery, Stoke Gabriel, Totnes, South Devon TQ9 6SL

Moira Pottery Co. Ltd, Moira, Burton-on-Trent, Staffs DE12 6DF

Morganite Thermal Ceramics, Liverpool Road, Neston, South Wirral, Cheshire L64 3RE

Pilling Pottery, School Lane, Pilling, Nr Garstang, Lancs PR3 6HB

Potclays Ltd, Brickkiln Lane, Etruria, Stoke-on-Trent, Staffs

Potterycrafts Ltd, Campbell Road, Stoke-on-Trent, Staffs ST4 4ET

Ratcliffe & Sons, Rope Street, Shelton New Road, Stoke-on-Trent, Staffs ST4 6DJ

Watts, Blake, Bearne & Co Plc, Courtenay Park, Newton Abbot, Devon TQ12 4PS

United States of America

A. D. Alpine Inc., 353 Coral Circle, El Segundo, California 90245

The Craftool Co. Inc., 142 West 240th Street, Harbor City, California 90710

Denver Fireclay Co., P.O. Box 5507, Denver, Colorado 80217

Ferro Corporation, 4150 East 56th Street, Cleveland, Ohio

Kentucky-Tennessee Clay Co., Box 417, Mayfield, Kentucky, Ohio 42066

Scargo Pottery, Dennis, Cape Cod, Massachusetts

Stewart Clay Co. Inc., 133 Mulberry Street, New York, NY 10013

United Clay Mines Corporation, 101 Oakland Street, Trenton, NJ 08606

Magazines

Excellent pottery magazines are published in Europe and the United States. The pioneer in Britain was *Ceramic Review*, at 21 Carnaby Street, London W1V 1PH; in America, *Ceramics Monthly*, 1609 Northwest Boulevard, Columbus, Ohio 43212 is recommended; and in France the excellent *Revue de la Ceramique et du Verre* is published from 61 Rue Marconi, 62880 Vendin-le-Vieil.

Glossary

Banding wheel or 'bench whirler'. An unpowered tabletop wheel on a spindle, used for painting horizontal bands on to pots, or to support hand-built pots in the making.

Bat Kiln shelf or a flat wooden surface to work on, which is portable.

Biscuit or Bisc. Unglazed porous pottery fired once.

Bloating Ugly blisters in the body of the pot which usually occur in the glaze firing. This is often due to carelessly mixed clays.

Body The word which all potters use for the clay from which pots are made.

Cottle A wall of clay, wood or linoleum used to surround the clay mould to prevent the liquid plaster from spilling.

Crawling This is when the glaze shrinks away from the body of the pot. Dust or grease on the pot can be the cause of this.

Deflocculant A substance which when added to thick slip, makes it much more runny. Two of these thinners are sodium silicate and sodium carbonate.

Earthenware Soft, porous, glazed pottery fired to a temperature of 1000–1100°C.

Felspar This mineral contains silica and alumina. It is the commonest ingredient in stoneware and porcelain glaze, as well as being a major constituent of clay.

Fettling Smoothing or trimming the surface of a hardening pot in preparation for firing.

Fireclay Refractory clays which withstand high temperatures, are yellow or grey in colour and are used for parts of kilns and bricks. They are too coarse for use in most domestic pottery.

Firing Placing the pottery in a kiln and heating it to a temperature to make it hard and permanent.

Flux A melting agent which causes silica to form glaze or glass.

Footring If the pot is raised from the surface on which it stands by a circle of clay at the base, this is called a footring. During the turning stage it is shaped and hollowed.

Frit Flux and silica are melted together and reground to a fine powder, making a glaze ingredient which has the same effect as, but avoids the toxicity of, raw fluxes such as lead.

Glaze A coating of glass applied to the surface of a pot. Silica melted with a flux, such as lead, sodium or potassium makes a glaze, and is often coloured with metal oxides.

Greenware The name applied to pots before they are fired.

Grog Ground-down fired pottery added to plastic clay gives texture and reduces shrinkage.

Grout Cement used to fill in joints between tiles.

Kidney A kidney-shaped metal or rubber tool used for finishing pots on the wheel, made in press-moulds or by hand.

Lawn A phosphor-bronze sieve with a fine mesh for sieving slips and glazes.

Leather-hard The state of clay which has partially dried, but which is still soft enough to work. Also described as cheese-hard.

Lugs Side projections on pots used as handles.

Majolica White tin-glazed earthenware, usually with painted designs in blue and other colours. The term originates from Majorca, and the style of pottery is also known as Delft ware.

On-glaze Decoration applied on top of an unfired glaze using metal oxides or prepared colourants.

Over-firing This usually refers to the glaze and often means that the pot has gained ugly characteristics from exceeding the optimum temperature. Over-fired pots often stick to the kiln shelves.

Oxidised Fired in a kiln with adequate oxygen leaving metallic colours bright. Oxygen is only required in kilns in which combustion occurs, i.e. gas or wood kilns. Electric kilns give oxidised results since there is no combustion.

Pinholing When gas bubbles out of the glaze it can cause masses of minute holes on the surface. Usually due to mineral impurities.

Plastic A plastic clay has the ability to be shaped easily and to retain its shape.

Plunge pots Simple pots formed around a dowel or block of wood and chopped or beaten into shape. Also called 'bashed' pots.

Porcelain White, often translucent stoneware made from a mixture of pure clays, with the addition of calcium for translucency.

Raw glazing The technique of applying glaze to an unfired pot and heating the clay and glaze together. Raw clay is unfired clay.

Reduced Fired in an oxygen-starved atmosphere which reduces the colour of metal oxides to their respective metal forms. Thus copper becomes coppery-red unlike the characteristic green of oxidised copper roofs.

Refractory The capacity of a material to withstand high temperatures in pottery. Clays suitable for stoneware and porcelain are described as refractory clays.

Saggar A fireclay box used in oil, gas or solid fuel-burning kilns to contain the pottery, thus protecting it from the flames.

Seger cone A pyroscope designed to indicate heat by melting and changing shape. They are small pyramids of glaze-like material which bend when the correct temperature is reached. They are placed in the kiln so that they can be seen through the spy-hole.

Sgraffito A decorative technique in which a sharp tool is used to scratch through a slip to clay below. The same technique is applied to glazed pottery, when designs are scratched through an unfired glaze to show a fired glaze below.

Silk-screen The application of design to a pot by pressing colours in a carrier medium through those parts of a fine screen which have not been blocked off with wax.

Slip Liquid clay in a non-plastic state, with the consistency of cream.

Slip-trailing Applying designs by passing clay through a nozzle attached to a small rubber bag, like icing a cake.

Slurry A mixture of clay and water. An alternative name for slip, but more commonly used when the mixture cements clay joins.

Soaking Leaving the kiln on at the firing's required temperature, for half an hour or so. Often improves the quality of the glaze.

Sprigging Taking small solid casts from moulds and fixing them to the surface of pots, usually of a different colour for contrast, as in edgwood Jasper ware.

Stoneware Glazed pottery fired to a temperature above 1200°C, when the body is vitrified.

Throwing Making pots with the hands from plastic clay on a wheel.

Turning Trimming thrown pots when they are leather-hard, using metal tools on a wheel.

Wad mill Another name for an extruder. The wad is simply the lump of clay which goes inside it.

Wedging The cutting and re-forming of plastic clay before kneading. This ensures an even texture. Many potters apply the term wedging to the kneading process as well.

Wheel A smoothly revolving platform powered either by the potter's legs or by electricity and capable of varied speeds of rotation.

Wheel head A circular flat disc on which the pot is formed. It is attached to the revolving spindle of the potter's wheel.

Acknowledgements

In getting together the many illustrations in this book the author would like to acknowledge the help received from many individual potters, and in particular from Deirdre Bowles, Suzy Corby, Julian Falk, Karen Foster, Bryan and Julia Newman, Les Sharp, Jane Waller, Michael Woods and Mead Pottery. The photographs are Alphabet and Image copyright with the exception of the following:

Ian Auld, page 101 (top); Gordon Baldwin, p. 125 (bottom); Alan Barrett-Danes, p. 48 (top); Val Barry, p. 116; Alison Britton, p. 108 (top); Deirdre Burnett, p. 85 (bottom); Alan Caiger-Smith, p. 124 (bottom); Crafts Advisory Committee, pp. 26 (bottom right), 110 (both), 119 (bottom right), 121 (top left), 129; David Cripps, p. 104; Dragon Ceramex, Congresbury, p. 112 (bottom); Ruth Duckworth, p. 108 (bottom); David Edmonds, p. 119 (bottom left); Everson Museum of Art, Syracuse, New York (*New Works in Clay*, 1976), pp. 94, 121 (top right); Jane Hamlyn, p. 122 (top right); Gerry Harvey, pp. 25, 70 (top left), 79 (bottom right); Michael Holford, pp. 57 (bottom), 67, 69 by courtesy of the Victoria and Albert Museum, London, 76 (bottom), 93, 103 (both), 126 (bottom); Roger Honey, p. 54 (top); Karen Karnes, p. 35 (top); Peter Kinnear, p. 59 (bottom); Dr Paul Koster Kunsthammer, pp. 42, 87 (top right); Lakeland Photographic, p. 115 (top); Bernard Leach, p. 75; Peter McCulloch, pp. 27, 37 (bottom); John Mennell, pp. 30 (bottom), 43 (top), 117 (bottom left), 122 (top left), 124 (top); Michael Moore, p. 127 (bottom left); Christine Poole, pp. 1, 120 (top), 127 (top right); Scott Creek Pottery, Davenport, USA, p. 113 (bottom); John Solly, p. 26 (top); © SPADEM, Paris 1978, p. 128 (left); Stafford College of Further Education, p. 53; Marianne de Trey, pp. 59 (top), 109 (top), 119 (top), 126 (top); University of Washington Press, p. 101 (bottom); John Weatherhill, Inc. (*The Art of Japanese Ceramics*), p. 68 (bottom); Eric Webster, pp. 4 (top), 81 (all), 85 (top), 86 (both), 87 (top left and bottom); Robin Welch, pp. 26 (bottom left), 49, 73 (top right); Charles Wharry, p. 128 (bottom); J. Coper 65, 130, 131.